M000227882

THE

HEALING

POWER OF

GOD

STAN JANTZ

HARVEST HOUSE PUBLISHERS
EUGENE, OREGON

Published in association with the literary agency of The Steve Laube Agency, LLC, 24 W. Camelback Rd. A-635, Phoenix, Arizona 85013.

For bulk, special sales, or ministry purchases, please call 1-800-547-8979. Email: Customerservice@hhpbooks.com

Cover by Studio Gearbox

Cover photo © Cat_arch_angel / Shutterstock; Qweek / istock

The Healing Power of God
Copyright © 2020 by Stan Jantz
Published by Harvest House Publishers
Eugene, Oregon 97408
www.harvesthousepublishers.com

Library of Congress Cataloging-in-Publication Data

Names: Jantz, Stan, - author.
Title: The healing power of God / Stan Jantz.
Description: Eugene, Oregon : Harvest House Publishers, 2020. | Summary:
   "The Healing Power of God will introduce you to Accounts of miracles
   both from biblical and present times The obstacles that can be keep us
   from taking the miraculous seriously The reason the presence of miracles
   is essential to your life-both now and in the future How you can
   experience God's healing touch and bring heaven to earth You are the
   child of a supernatural God; yours is a supernatural journey. You don't
   have to wait for heaven to experience God's miraculous and wonderous
   power"—Provided by publisher.
Identifiers: LCCN 2020012298 (print) | LCCN 2020012299 (ebook) | ISBN
   9780736977838 (trade paperback) | ISBN 9780736977845 (ebook)
Subjects: LCSH: Miracles. | Healing—Religious aspects—Christianity.
Classification: LCC BT97.3 .J36 2020 (print) | LCC BT97.3 (ebook) | DDC
   231.7/3—dc23
LC record available at https://lccn.loc.gov/2020012298
LC ebook record available at https://lccn.loc.gov/2020012299

Printed in the United States of America

20 21 22 23   24 25 26 27 28   / VP-RD / 10 9 8 7 6 5 4 3 2 1

Contents

Introduction

Do you believe in miracles?

The first time I heard that question wasn't in church or a revival meeting or a healing service. It was in 1980 as I was watching a television broadcast of the Olympic hockey game between the USA's team of amateur college players and the mighty Soviet Union.

In what has become known as the Miracle on Ice, the match featured a young and unknown Al Michaels as the play-by-play announcer. When the final buzzer sounded, it was official. The Americans had pulled off the unexpected, the unlikely, and even the miraculous. As the team of young hockey players celebrated with upraised arms and expressions of amazement, Michaels uttered the question that would cement his place in broadcasting history and forever become the catch phrase for the unexpected, the unlikely, and even the miraculous coming true.

Since that historic night, I have heard the question, "Do you believe in miracles?" many times, but never in any meaningful context. If anything, the question has become part of the American can-do spirit rather than about our spiritual sensibilities.

I haven't heard the question in any church I have attended. No pastor has ever asked me if I believe in miracles, either from the pulpit or in casual conversation. I'm not saying the pastors I have known do not believe in miracles. Of course they do! They are Christians, so they must believe. Miracles are a key feature of the faith they espouse and the Bible they teach.

So why don't Christian leaders ask the question?

Should we assume that people who go to church automatically believe in miracles? I suppose you could make a case that the Christian faith and miracles go together like peanut butter and jelly. But do people who believe in God and claim to follow Jesus Christ really believe in miracles? Do they really believe in the healing power of God? And if they say yes to these questions, what kind of miracles and what kind of healing do they believe in?

If we're talking about an underdog defeating a champion, then it's not a stretch to say we believe in miracles. How about finding a parking space at Trader Joe's on a Saturday morning? Plenty of people—even those with no church affiliation—would utter the words, "It's a miracle" upon finding a premium parking spot in front of a busy store like Trader Joe's.

But what about a miracle like the ones contained in the Bible? The parting of the Red Sea in front of two million Israelites fleeing the Egyptian army? The prophet Elijah going to heaven in a chariot of fire? Jesus calming the sea with just a word? Lazarus being raised from the dead? Do we believe these aberrations of nature could occur today?

And what about the healings described in the New Testament, especially the ones performed by Jesus? The deaf man who hears, the blind man who sees, the woman who stops bleeding after twelve years, the crippled man who walks—all of them healed instantly. These are the kinds of miracles that are almost routine in the life of Christ and the apostles. Do they happen today? Do we believe they *could* happen?

If you're like me, you hear stories and rumors of people today being healed, but have you witnessed such a miracle with your own eyes? Have you seen a crippled person stand up and walk because someone said, "Rise and be healed"? Have you watched as a person born blind suddenly has sight because someone uttered the words, "In the name of Jesus be healed"? I will admit to you that I have never seen such a thing.

Admitting this to you at the beginning of a book on the healing power of God may not be the best strategy, especially if you are deciding whether to keep reading. But I might as well get it out in the open so you can either stop reading because you have concluded I have no credibility or you will continue reading because you can identify with what I'm saying.

If you're in the second group—those who will keep reading—I invite you to continue with me on this journey of discovery because we have something in common. We want to believe in miracles that are greater than the Olympic hockey game or the unlikely parking spot or the brilliant sunset that makes us all warm and fuzzy inside. We want to believe that God heals today, though maybe not exactly as he did in the Bible.

We want to answer the question, "Do you believe in miracles?" with a resounding *yes*. We want to believe that God still heals today because, well, we all know a lot of people who could use a good, honest healing right about now. We want to believe that God still heals and miracles still happen, but not because we wish it were true. We want to believe because it's absolutely true.

The Healing Power of God

The title of this book and its subtitle—*A Biblical Embrace of the Supernatural*—suggest two important things. First, as much as we all want to believe in miracles, what we really care about is God's healing power. Because we live in a world characterized by brokenness, there is perhaps no greater longing in our world today than the desire for healing—whether physical, emotional, or spiritual.

Second, there is a deep fascination in our culture with the supernatural. On the one hand you see the supernatural packaged in popular media, where the heroes are invariably *super* heroes. On the other hand, you have Christians who believe in a supernatural God who has acted miraculously in history, but they seem a little embarrassed to be talking about a supernatural God with their neighbors.

My hope is that *The Healing Power of God* will bridge this supernatural chasm by showing that miracles and healing are not only real but also essential to our lives both now and in the future. As we go on this journey of discovery together, here is what you can expect.

The healing power of God falls under the umbrella of his miraculous power, so in chapter 1 we will look at what a miracle really is. We will consider what credible philosophers, theologians, and researchers have concluded about miracles, and then compare their perspectives with Scripture.

Chapter 2 will explore the reasons we don't take miracles seriously. You would expect this chapter to focus exclusively on unbelievers, but people who believe in God sometimes have just as big a problem with miracles as those who don't.

The Bible is full of miracles—231 by one count. In chapter 3 we will answer the question, "Why are there so many miracles in the Bible?" And then we will look at the three Greatest Miracles in the Bible—without which none of the other miracles would exist or even be possible.

Chapter 4 talks about miracles—especially healings—going on today. If you're like I am, you may be skeptical about some of these stories because they just seem too good to be true. Or too crazy. But that's not God's fault. The reasons for his healing haven't changed from the Bible times to today. Therefore, the purpose of this chapter is to discover why God heals.

Chapter 5 may be the toughest chapter to read—it certainly was the most difficult for me to write—because it considers the fact that God doesn't always heal. Of course, we *hope* he will heal, but sometimes he doesn't. We all know people who suffer and die with no intervention from God.

There are times when we long for God's healing touch. Every one of us knows someone right now who needs a true healing. I have someone in mind, and it's likely you do as well. Chapter 6 will reveal why this longing is profound and universal and whether we can and should believe that healing is possible today.

If we truly believe in a supernatural God, it's not too big a leap to believe in the supernatural acts of God. And since God is ever present in our world, chapter 7 will consider how those of us who live by faith can live supernaturally in a world that is anchored in the natural. We will do this by providing a thirty-day devotional that will help you apply God's miracles and healing touch to your own life and the lives of those around you today.

By the time you finish this book, I hope you will understand the reason why there are miracles in our world, and why you can have confidence they are as real today as they were in Bible times. As for God's healing touch, it's likely you already believe it's possible, but you're not quite sure it can happen to you or someone you love and care about.

Honestly, that's the primary reason I decided to write *The*

Healing Power of God. I am honored that you have chosen to travel this journey of supernatural discovery with me. By the time we're done with this book, I hope and pray that we will understand and then live with the reality that the Christian life is much more than another belief system that is true but has no transcendent power. Much more than that, our life with God is a supernatural one, characterized by the love, compassion, and power of God.

A Biblical Embrace of the Supernatural

My journey to embrace the supernatural life I have been given by God began when I explored the origin of my earthly life. Until recently, I knew very little about the story of my father's encounter with healing and how the outcome charted the course of my life. As I uncovered the details through forgotten letters and an interview with his lone remaining sibling, it was as if the supernatural life God designed for me all along suddenly opened up.

Even though I have written a book about God's healing power and the supernatural life he wants us to live, I am still getting to know what it's like to know what the Bible says about miracles and healing and how I can apply that to my life. As you experience this book and explore the Scriptures and books referenced throughout, may you likewise begin to live a life fully alive in the healing power of our loving and gracious God.

CHAPTER 1

What Is a Miracle?

My first encounter with miracles and healing came when I was two years old. My father was diagnosed with Hodgkin's disease, commonly known in those days as "young man's disease" because the most common victims were males between the ages of fifteen and thirty-five. My father was twenty-four when he was given the diagnosis.

My mother wanted him to immediately see a doctor and get treatment. But my father was hesitant, not because he didn't trust the medical profession but because he believed he was going to be healed, and he didn't want to demonstrate a lack of faith.

At the time this drama was unfolding, my father was studying for the ministry at Wheaton College in the suburbs of Chicago. My father came out of the Christian and Missionary Alliance tradition, so at that time our little family of three was attending Southside Alliance Church in Chicago, where the legendary A. W. Tozer was the pastor. Tozer was known as a deeply spiritual man who taught that every Christian should long for the "manifest presence of God." Writing in his classic book *The Pursuit of God*, first published in 1948, Tozer expressed what my father must have felt. I have no doubt my father read these words from Tozer's best-known book:

> I want deliberately to encourage this mighty longing after God. The lack of it has brought us to our present low estate. The stiff and wooden quality about our religious lives is a result of our lack of holy desire. Complacency is a deadly foe of all spiritual growth. Acute desire must be present or there will be no manifestation of Christ to His people. He waits to be wanted. Too bad that with many of us He waits so long, so very long, in vain.[1]

I believe the greatest desire of my father's heart was to long after God, to experience the manifest presence of Christ in his life. Therefore, when he was diagnosed with a life-threatening disease, his first inclination was not to seek an earthly remedy but to go straight to his heavenly Father. And in the Spirit, he boldly asked Dr. Tozer to pray for his healing.

My father's older brother, Sam, who was also studying for the ministry, went with my father to Tozer's home. There was great expectancy that God was about to do a miracle. I have a letter written by my uncle Sam to their parents expressing the fervency with which Tozer prayed. He laid his hands on my father and asked God to heal him. I can only imagine the divine power my father must have felt.

If we're going to talk about healing, we have to first talk about miracles, since healing is a kind of miracle. And sometimes it's easier to begin a conversation with someone about miracles rather than about healing. Talking about healing can sometimes make people nervous, but everyone can relate to a miracle because miracles make people feel good. The prospect that miracles are possible gives hope to all people—those who believe in God as well as those who don't.

According to a survey by Barna Research, two-thirds of Americans believe people can be physically healed supernaturally by God. Nearly 70 percent have prayed for someone to be healed, and among committed Christians, 75 percent believe they have actually witnessed a miracle. Perhaps the most astonishing statistic is that more than half of all physicians say they have seen a miracle in the course of their practice.[2]

So there's no crisis of belief when it comes to miracles and healing. But there is a lack of clarity and consensus as to what a miracle really is. It's common for people to "feel" the miraculous in various experiences: a sunset, the stars, a newborn baby. Corporations have even used the word to describe popular products, such as fake mayonnaise (Miracle Whip) and lawn fertilizer (Miracle Gro). There's just one problem. None of these miracle feelings or objects are actually a miracle.

There is no shortage of definitions for *miracle*, probably because, as Eric Metaxas writes in his book *Miracles*, "what is and what isn't a miracle is extremely subjective."[3] Metaxas may have a point, especially when you include in the mix definitions by skeptics. For example, the philosopher David Hume famously hated the idea of miracles, but he defined them anyway as a violation of natural law.

You might read that and say to yourself, that sounds about right. Logic dictates that Jesus walking on the water would seem to violate the laws of nature, as would the resurrection of Jesus from the dead, since it's natural for a person to sink in water and a dead person to stay dead. But are such occurrences a violation of natural law or simply an interruption?

I BELIEVE IN MIRACLES...SORT OF

Before I get into definitions some really smart people have come up with, I have a confession to make. I believe in God and the supernatural because I have experienced a spiritual transformation that can only be described as supernatural. My spiritual rebirth didn't happen as a result of my own effort or any other natural means but by the grace of God. My "conversion" happened when I was seven years old, so you could say I have lived a supernatural life for most of my life. Only it hasn't always felt that way.

Since I'm confessing here, I will be transparent with you. I have never *felt* I was living a supernatural life. I know in my head that God is real, but I don't wake up in the morning thinking, *Wow, I'm going to encounter the miraculous today because I believe in a supernatural God.* I believe in God and have put my faith in him, but it is a practical faith. Beyond believing that the supernatural exists and miracles are real, my actions and my words don't show that I truly believe *in* the supernatural, and I even wonder sometimes if I will ever see a true miracle.

I had to get that off my chest. I could not go on with this book on the healing power of God if I did not first confess this to you. So why did I write this book? For one basic reason: I want to experience the supernatural. I want to see a miracle. I want to feel God's touch. Perhaps just like you, I have a longing to see the evidence that God is active in the world and that he hasn't forgotten about us.

I mentioned David Hume (1711–1776), a Scottish philosopher who lived and wrote at a time in history known as the Age of Enlightenment (or the Age of Reason). It all started with the French philosopher René Descartes (1596–1650), who proposed that in order to figure out the world, all you need is reason.

Before Descartes, the consensus was that you needed faith to believe in God.

In England, Sir Isaac Newton (1642–1727) contributed massively to advancements in science and math that seemed to unlock the secrets of the natural world. His astounding discoveries advanced the Enlightenment in both Europe and the American colonies. As the eighteenth century unfolded, the leading thinkers of the world were convinced that reason and reason alone was the key to the universe and to belief in God.

The Enlightenment captured America's founding fathers, in particular Benjamin Franklin and Thomas Jefferson. They accepted that God created the universe, but they didn't believe God was active in the world. He existed but was perfectly willing to let the universe run on its own. This view of God is known as *deism,* wherein God exists but is not personal. And because God is not involved in history or in the lives of individuals, it's up to us to make our own way through reason and effort. (By contrast, the belief that God created the world and is personally involved with it is called *theism.*)

Any notion of God interfering with the fine work of human agents was out of the question. So naturally the idea that God would interrupt or intervene in the world was not only impossible but also repugnant. That's why Thomas Jefferson, the primary writer of the Declaration of Independence, believed that God existed but without the miraculous interfering with our world. Jefferson famously produced a New Testament with all the supernatural elements removed. He was fine with the teachings of Jesus but could not condone his miracles.

By no stretch of the imagination do I share David Hume's and Thomas Jefferson's skepticism about the miraculous. But if

I am being completely honest (something I will continue to be throughout the book), I will confess that I have been skeptical at times when I hear or read about miracles occurring, whether here in my home city, state, and country, or in other countries, especially in the Global South. Maybe it's because I have lived my Christian life almost exclusively through the lens of Western culture and theology. Perhaps my mild skepticism is due to my conservative church upbringing. More likely, it's a combination of both.

But does that get me off the hook? Am I being faithful to the God who saved me if I take an ostrich view of miracles and bury my head in the sand of conservative theological tradition? Or do I look to the hills, from where my help comes, and acknowledge that by denying or even ignoring the presence of miracles—and by implication the supernatural—in the world, I am turning my back to the reality of the spectacular, incredible, mind-bending miracles that we read about in the pages of Scripture?

And still I wonder. Do those kinds of miracles occur today? *Can* they occur today? We're going to find out as this book unfolds. But for now, let's explore what a miracle really is.

IN SEARCH OF A DEFINITION

The first book I ever read on miracles was the celebrated book by C.S. Lewis titled, appropriately enough, *Miracles.* First published in 1947, *Miracles* has been the standard bearer for this topic ever since. It's not an easy book to get through, but it's well worth the effort. Lewis' discussion of "Nature" or the natural world and its relationship to the supernatural is brilliant.

Lewis uses the word *miracle* to mean "an interference with Nature by supernatural power."[4] He contends that miracles are possible only if "there exists, in addition to Nature, something else which we call the supernatural."[5] Together, naturalism and supernaturalism give us a composite picture of reality. However, the naturalist believes that the world we see "exists on its own in space and time, and that nothing else exists." By comparison,

> The Supernaturalist believes that one Thing exists on its own and has produced the framework or space and time and the procession of systematically connected events which fill them. This framework, and this filling, he calls Nature. It may, or may not, be the only reality which the one Primary Thing has produced. There might be other systems in addition to the one we call Nature.[6]

If nature is the only thing that's true, says Lewis, then miracles are impossible. But if supernaturalism is also true, then miracles are possible. But that doesn't mean the two—naturalism and supernaturalism—exist in separate worlds. They aren't mutually exclusive. In fact, they are inextricably connected.

"All records of miracles teach the same thing," writes Lewis. They elicit "fear and wonder (that is what the very word *miracle* implies) among the spectators, and are taken as evidence of supernatural power. If they were not known to be contrary to the laws of nature how could they suggest the presence of the supernatural?"[7]

Lewis uses the example of the virgin birth, a pivotal belief in Christianity. Even by the standards of scientific knowledge in the first century, Mary's fiancé, Joseph, knew there was only one way for a woman to become pregnant. When Mary told Joseph she was going to have a baby, he assumed the natural explanation for her pregnancy and decided to break the engagement because, well, wasn't it obvious he wasn't the father?

What Joseph didn't know (an angel had to explain it to him) was that God had interrupted the natural process of human conception to accomplish what was scientifically impossible. To put it simply, God performed a miracle. And so you have the simplest definition of a miracle, proposed quite nicely by Norman Geisler: "A miracle is a special act of God that interrupts the natural course of events."[8]

There are two components of this definition that impact the way we look at miracles today. First is the relationship of the miracle to the "natural course of events." The way Jesus came into the world—through the virgin birth—was impossible unless the regular process of nature was, to quote Lewis again, "over-ruled or supplemented by something from beyond nature."[9] In fact, if this miracle (or any miracle for that matter) was not an interruption of the laws of nature, it could not be called a miracle. Indeed, the evidence of supernatural power is what makes something miraculous.

That's why a sunset or the birth of a baby are not miraculous because they are perfectly natural. That's not to say such things are incapable of evoking wonder at God's goodness, power, and beauty, but they are not miracles in the true sense of the word.

The second part of the definition of miracle is this: In order for us to perceive anything as a miracle, we need to know the rules of nature. As Lewis puts it,

> Nothing can seem extraordinary until you have discovered what is ordinary. Belief in miracles, far from depending on an ignorance of the laws of nature, is only possible in so far as those laws are known.[10]

THE SUPERNATURAL POWER OF GOD

Here's what has struck me as I have been working on this book. By his supernatural power, God created a world for us to inhabit that is spectacular and unbelievably intricate and complex. Even the ancients, without the benefit of scientific knowledge as we have today, marveled at the way the universe works. Writing three thousand years ago, David observed,

> The heavens proclaim the glory of God.
>   The skies display his craftsmanship.
> Day after day they continue to speak;
>   night after night they make him known.
> They speak without a sound or word;
>   their voice is never heard.
> Yet their message has gone throughout the earth,
>   and their words to all the world.
>   (Psalm 19:1-4)

And two thousand years ago the apostle Paul wrote,

> For ever since the world was created, people have seen the earth and sky. Through everything God made, they can clearly see his invisible qualities— his eternal power and divine nature. So they have no excuse for not knowing God (Romans 1:20).

If you see the world only from the natural perspective, with no accounting for a Creator who exists outside nature, who is the First Cause of everything that exists, the only conclusion is that the universe came about by natural means. Either it has always existed, or it has generated itself, or it is the result of some alien being (though certainly not God).

This is nothing new. People have long invented alternate explanations, whether gods or aliens, to avoid the idea that a transcendent God exists outside of our material existence and that this immaterial God created our material world. As the writer of Hebrews observes, God brought everything into existence out of nothing by the power of his creative and awesome word:

> By faith we understand that the entire universe was formed at God's command, that what we now see did not come from anything that can be seen (Hebrews 11:3)

With all this in mind, can you see why some people try so hard to disbelieve in miracles? If a miracle is a special act of God that interrupts the natural course of events, you have to accept the reality that God exists in the first place. And not just any God, but the God of the Bible, who is described as—

- eternal (Psalm 90:2)
- infinite (Revelation 1:8)
- holy (Isaiah 6:3)
- just (Deuteronomy 32:4)
- all powerful (Revelation 19:6)
- all knowing (Psalm 139:1-4)
- always present (Psalm 139:7-12)
- love (1 John 4:7-9)

THE GOD WHO ACTS IN HISTORY

The late Richard Purtill, who taught philosophy at Western

Washington University, takes Lewis's basic definition of *miracle* and expands it: "A miracle is an event in which God temporarily makes an exception to the natural order of things, to show that God is acting."

This definition reminds us that a miracle is an event brought about by God's power. "If for some reason," writes Purtill, "we find that some apparently wonderful event can be accounted for by some power less than the power of God, then we withhold the designation *miracle*."[11]

Geisler agrees that a miracle shows us that God is acting in history, and he explains why: "To glorify God and to provide evidence for God's people to believe."[12]

When God created the universe, he did it with us in mind. He made a world and a planet—the Bible refers to these as "the heavens and the earth"—ideally suited for life, in particular for the life of humanity. God created people "in his image," which means we are like God in terms of our personality and certain traits: love, care, creativity, and the ability to be generative. But we don't share God's supernatural characteristics and abilities—in particular his "omni" attributes (omnipotence, omniscience, and omnipresence). However, we are not finite beings. As Lewis reminds us, we are more than mere mortals:

> There are no ordinary people. You have never talked to a mere mortal. Nations, cultures, arts, civilizations —these are mortal, and their life is to ours as the life of a gnat. But it is immortals whom we joke with, work with, marry, snub and exploit—immortal horrors or everlasting splendors.[13]

God is more than a mere mortal as well, but he is much

more. In addition to being immortal, God is eternal and immaterial and everywhere at once. He isn't the universe, but he fills the created world with his presence and power. As the psalmist David writes,

> I can never escape from your Spirit!
>   I can never get away from your presence!
> If I go up to heaven, you are there;
>   if I go down to the grave, you are there.
> If I ride the wings of the morning,
>   if I dwell by the farthest oceans,
> even there your hand will guide me,
>   and your strength will support me.
>
> (Psalm 139:7-10)

There's another important quality we possess that God does not: we have the ability to sin. It's part of the free will God built into our DNA. God gave our first parents, Adam and Eve, and every human born since then the choice to follow or reject him. The original plan was for humanity to live in the garden as sinless immortal beings, never to die. But all that changed when Adam and Eve chose to follow their own way rather than God.

It's not as if Adam and Eve didn't know the consequences of this decision. God told them they were free to eat of any tree in the garden, including the tree of life. "But you must not eat from the tree of the knowledge of good and evil," God warned, "for when you eat from it you will certainly die" (Genesis 2:17 NIV).

In our original immortal state before sin entered the world, the supernatural was an integral and visible part of the natural world God created. The narrative in Genesis makes reference to God "walking in the garden in the cool of the day" (Genesis 3:8 NIV). From the beginning, God intended his human creation to live with him in the abundant and beautiful natural world he created with the presence of the supernatural as natural as breathing. The natural and supernatural existed together and in harmony. Material beings interacted with the immaterial God. There were no miracles because all of life existed in this beautiful blend of the natural and supernatural.

WHY GOD STARTED DOING MIRACLES

When temptation entered the world, sin followed, upsetting the beautiful balance and harmony of natural and supernatural existing together. At that moment humanity and the natural world changed, and with it our relationship with the supernatural. Because sin now existed in God's once-perfect natural world, the relationship between a holy God and sinful humanity changed.

No longer would God walk with humanity in the cool of the day. The natural world would continue to exist, but not without the effect of sin. Rather than operating in perfect and unbroken harmony, the natural world began "groaning as in the pains of childbirth," something it has continued to do to the present time (Romans 8:22). The supernatural world still exists, but it is not immediately present in our natural world, and its effects are not constantly in front of us.

But that's not the end of the story. Because of God's extraordinary love for us, he put a rescue plan into action the moment we rejected him. The apostle Paul gives us the highlights of this plan in his letter to the church at Ephesus. Designed "before the creation of the world," this plan centered on Jesus Christ, who would take on the punishment we deserved and forgive our sins "in accordance with the riches of God's grace that he lavished on us." It would be "put into effect when the times reach their fulfillment—to bring unity to all things in heaven and on earth under Christ" (Ephesians 1:3-10 NIV). Jesus would become the intermediary between God and man, restoring the intimacy and harmony that once existed in the garden.

Until that time reached its fulfillment (Galatians 4:4), God called out a people to become the channel for his plan. Through the physical existence of these chosen people would come the Savior of the world, the one promised by God before the beginning, who would bring the supernatural and the natural world together. During this time, God revealed himself selectively and in various ways through miracles, bringing the supernatural into the natural world to advance his purposes and to remind his people that he is God and above him is no other.

God called prophets and gave them power, he defeated the enemies of his people, and he healed his people to remind them that the Savior, the Messiah, his very Son would be coming as the ultimate miracle worker and healer because he would be God himself in human form.

HEAVEN CAME TO EARTH

So Jesus came to earth, God descending in human form to live among us for a while, once again uniting heaven and earth. Just as God did from heaven, Jesus did on earth. He brought the supernatural to the natural, doing everything God did. He called the apostles and gave them power, defeated the spiritual enemies of humanity, and conquered sickness—all because of his love, compassion, and power. Jesus also suffered on our behalf because of our sins, forgave us, and conquered the grave. By dying and coming back to life, Jesus gave us a preview of what we can expect in our future immortal lives, if we put our trust in him.

Sin and Satan and suffering still exist, but the supernatural life and healing touch of Jesus are stronger than these, present in our world today through the Holy Spirit, who is the presence of Christ in us. The supernatural and natural once again dwell together in each person who has been miraculously transformed by the person and work of Jesus.

We don't have to cry to heaven in our distress and hope that God hears us and descends with miraculous power. He has already done that through Jesus. The supernatural dwells in us because of his grace, forgiveness, love, and power.

So how should we live? As believers, we have two choices. We can live *naturally*, our heads filled with knowledge and principles for living because we follow sound Bible teaching and do our best to apply these principles to our lives. Or we can live *supernaturally*, still doing what God tells us to do in his world and in our hearts, but also living in the reality that the supernatural power of God is in us at all times.

Before Jesus came, God dwelled supernaturally in the temple. But because of what Jesus accomplished through his life, death, and resurrection, we are his temple. Rather than dwelling in a building made by human hands, God now dwells supernaturally in us. As we continue in our journey to discover how to live supernaturally in a natural world, this reality will take on more significance. Right now, let's find out why miracles are central to God's very existence.

WHY MIRACLES AND HEALING MATTER

Here's a quick review of our definition of a miracle, pulled from C. S. Lewis and others:

A miracle is an event in which God temporarily

interrupts the ordinary course of nature to show that
God has acted and continues to act in history.

From this definition, we can come to another conclusion:
miracles and healing are necessary to show God's activity in the
world. In fact, according to Geisler, there is no way to show that
Christianity is true "unless miracles are possible and actual."[14] We
can talk all day about how we believe in the God of the Bible and
offer all kinds of reasons why we think he is real. But without the
miraculous, Christianity is no better than any other belief system.

If you think I'm pushing this argument too far, here's what
the apostle Paul said about people who believe in a God devoid
of the miraculous:

> If Christ has not been raised, then your faith is use-
> less and you are still guilty of your sins. In that case,
> all who have died believing in Christ are lost! And if
> our hope in Christ is only for this life, we are more
> to be pitied than anyone in the world (1 Corinthi-
> ans 15:17-19).

In this indictment, Paul is referring to one particular miracle, the resurrection of Jesus Christ from the dead. There's a
reason why he picked this one as the "do or die" miracle to rep-
resent the entirety of the Christian faith. Even if you accept all
the other miracles and healings in the Bible as true, if this one
miracle didn't happen, the rest don't matter for one simple reason. Everything hinges on Jesus. If he is still dead, then God is
dead, and the best we can say is that he had a good run, creating
the universe and entering the world in human form to solve the
sin problem and all that. But he stumbled as he rounded the cor-
ner for the finish line.

But Paul believed in the resurrection because he was personally confronted by the resurrected Christ, as were more than five hundred other eyewitnesses (1 Corinthians 15:3-7), prompting him to declare, "But truth is that Christ *has* been raised up, the first in a long legacy of those who are going to leave the cemeteries" (1 Corinthians 15:20 MSG).

As we close this chapter, I need to continue my pattern of complete transparency. I am writing this book for those who believe God exists, whether you call yourself a Christian, a believer, a Christ follower, or a spiritual person. You're not a skeptic when it comes to belief in a supernatural God. Consequently, I'm not going to spend any time offering reasons why you can believe God exists.

What I want to do is show that it's reasonable to believe in miracles, and not just the miracles found in the Bible. As Geisler writes, "If God exists, we should come to human history with the expectation of the miraculous, not with a naturalistic bias against it."[15]

Expecting miracles in human history is not limited to the past. History is still being written, and God is just as involved in human affairs now as he was in the beginning. He is not detached but intensely interested in our lives. In fact, if you have committed to live in the truth of his redemption plan and have been transformed by the person and work of Jesus, then God loves being involved in every part of your life—emotional, spiritual, and physical. Here's how the psalmist David expresses this reality:

> The LORD directs the steps of the godly.
> He delights in every detail of their lives.
> (Psalm 37:23)

Knowing this should give us confidence that he cares when

we (or a loved one) are hurting, and that he desires to help and heal us. And yet we are sometimes hesitant and temper our expectations when it comes to miracles and healing. Why do we do this? Why do we sometimes doubt that God is willing and able to do the miraculous and heal us? That's the subject of the next chapter.

CHAPTER 2

Why Don't We Take Miracles and Healing Seriously?

When my father left A.W. Tozer's house, having been the object of a powerful prayer for his healing, he must have been euphoric. I certainly would have been. Of course, I was just two years old at the time, so I can only speculate. But I do know the sequence of events that followed that prayer.

According to my aunt Ruth, who at ninety-two is my father's only surviving sibling, my father was so convinced that he was going to be healed that he approached the administration at Wheaton College to ask if he could speak in chapel before the entire student body and faculty. I have my father's yearbook from that time at Wheaton. I can see the faces of the students and the professors. They stare back at me from the pages, lacking expression. But I can imagine the look on my father's face as he spoke.

"I will not die," he boldly declared, "but declare the glory of the Lord." His face must have been glowing as he spoke. "I know God wants to deliver me."

In fact, my father did die. He was not healed. No doubt the students and faculty were saddened. Perhaps only those who truly believed he would be healed were disappointed, but there was sadness enough to go around. My mother never spoke of the Wheaton declaration nor did she share with me the details of his illness.

The reason, I have learned from my aunt, is that my father's talk of healing upset my mother. And when he died, there was a breach with his extended family. As far as I know, the breach was never mended because my mother never adequately dealt with the loss of her husband, this young man who believed with all his heart that God would heal him.

I believe there are two reasons why people struggle to believe in miracles and healing. Some discount miracles and healing because admitting their possibility would imply the existence of God. Short of that, they would be forced to acknowledge that God is not detached from our world but is very much involved.

Others, like my mother, struggle because they have been let down. Maybe they prayed for healing and nothing happened. Or they watched someone else believe wholeheartedly that a miracle would occur, and God was silent.

C.S. Lewis wrote the definitive book on miracles, but when he was confronted with the loss of his dear wife, Joy, he struggled as any of us would and asked a question many of us have pondered: "Why is He so present a commander in our time of prosperity and so very absent a help in time of trouble."[1]

THE PROVIDENCE OF GOD

Perhaps as a result of losing her beloved, my mother's belief in the miraculous was tempered to the point that she commonly used the term *providential* to describe God's involvement in her life. That's not necessarily a negative reaction. Theologians use *providence* to describe God's continuous involvement in the daily events of the world (in general) and in our lives (in particular) to bring about his intended results. As we have already discussed, God is not like some absentee landlord who never bothers to know what is going on with his property. He is involved in the world and in the lives of those who have a relationship with him.

There is a preservation aspect to God's providence. This involves protection and providing for our needs, including

- creation as a whole (Nehemiah 9:6)
- our material needs (Matthew 6:25-26)
- our relationship with God (Romans 8:38-39)

God's providence doesn't protect us from dangers or problems. God never promises that we will avoid tragedy, suffering, or persecution. In fact, following God usually involves a degree of hardship, but these allow us to identify with Christ's sufferings (1 Peter 4:12-13).

I identify with the providence of God. Maybe it's because I heard my mother talk that way, but I also think it's the most common way Christians think about God's intervention in the world and in our lives. Even though we know in our heads that the supernatural world exists, our faith has become pragmatic. We may call something miraculous, but what we really mean is that God uses ordinary, natural means to get things done, including healing our bodies.

Theologian Winfried Corduan calls this "direct nonmiraculous intervention" and gives this example:

> Believers may say that God has acted in answering

> prayer, even when the answer to prayer followed completely natural and unsurprising processes. "I prayed for a good job, applied for this position and was hired."[2]

My mother would have said that such an outcome was providential. In reality, as Corduan points out, it's nothing more than "the coming together of a number of events that are in themselves physically possible (perhaps even somewhat probable) to form a constellation of events that is highly improbable."[3]

Because we believe that God acts on our behalf, we are comfortable concluding that God is behind a particular "constellation of events." But to believe that God would suddenly interrupt the natural flow of circumstances, events, or individual physical conditions to bring about a result that can only be called a true miracle—that is another thing entirely.

CHARACTERISTICS OF A TRUE MIRACLE

How do we move from only seeing God acting providentially to experiencing his miraculous and healing power? In my view, we need to get good at recognizing the miraculous going on all around us. It starts with observing God acting directly in some way. There is no absolute test when this occurs. We just need to be open to the characteristics of a true miracle. I found at least five:

1. A true miracle shows us God's power and compassion.

2. A true miracle brings good to the natural world.

3. A true miracle never has a relapse.

4. A true miracle occurs only according to God's will.

5. A true miracle always brings glory to God.

Here are two miracles recorded in the Bible—one in the Old Testament and one in the New—that fit these criteria.

The Widow at Zarephath (1 Kings 17:8-24)

God directed the prophet Elijah to the home of a widow who was to feed him. Only there had been no rain in the land so there was no food. Elijah declared that the meager supplies of flour and oil the widow did have would not be used up, and so there was food for Elijah and the woman and her family. Then the widow's son died, and Elijah prayed that the boy's life would return to him. When she saw that her son was alive, the widow declared, "Now I know for sure that you are a man of God, and that the LORD truly speaks through you" (v. 24). This is the first miracle in the Bible where someone was raised from the dead.

The Wedding at Cana (John 2:1-11)

Jesus and his disciples were invited to a wedding where the wine ran out, creating a huge embarrassment for the family of the wedding party. Jesus' mother informed Jesus of the problem, and he promptly asked the servants to fill six stone jars with water and draw some out for the master of the banquet to taste. Not realizing what had happened, he told the bridegroom, "A host always serves the best wine first. Then, when everyone has had a lot to drink, he brings out the less expensive wine. But you have kept the best until now!" (v. 10). The apostle John was there to observe this, and he wrote, "This miraculous sign at Cana in Galilee was the first time Jesus revealed his glory. And his disciples believed in him" (v. 11).

These are just two of the 231 miracles recorded in the Bible.

We accept these and other miracles in the Bible as true for the following reasons. Let's call this the chain of reasonable belief:

- Because we believe that a supernatural God exists, we expect him to do miracles.

- Because we believe that God is all powerful, we accept that God is able to perform miracles.

- Because we believe God is all knowing, we trust that God should know when and under what circumstances a miracle should occur.

- Because we believe God is all good and compassionate, we believe he has the desire to perform miracles on our behalf.

WHY I STRUGGLED TO BELIEVE

Those of us who trust in God and believe the Bible have no trouble accepting these miracles as historically true. And yet when it comes to our lives in the here and now, this chain of belief is broken in most of us. It was certainly broken in my mother and in me. I believed the miracles in the Bible because I believed in an all-powerful, all-knowing, all-benevolent God, but I didn't believe the miracles in the Bible could happen today. I believed that God could raise the dead and Jesus could turn water into wine, but I didn't think miracles and healings like these were possible in my time.

Why did I think this way? As I have examined my own thinking and my own heart, I have identified three factors that have shaped my perspective on miracles and healing today.

I Was Biased Against the Supernatural

This has been one of the great paradoxes of my life. Even though I have always believed in a supernatural God, I didn't believe he acted in real time to do miracles like the ones I saw in the Bible. On the surface, this may seem like a direct contradiction to Christian belief, but when I dug a little deeper, it made perfect sense. Here's why.

After my father died, I was raised in a church tradition that did not talk much about the supernatural. I was taught that when it comes to miracles, God no longer behaves as he did in the Old and New Testaments. I didn't know it then, but I have discovered that this teaching has a label. It's known as the "cessationist" view of God and Scripture. What this means is that God performed miracles at various times for specific reasons throughout history, but he has "ceased" to do miracles like that today. I know, it sounds a little crazy, but stay with me for a moment.

When you read the Bible, you can see clusters of miracles at certain times. According to cessationist belief, there are three such clusters:

1. The Mosaic period, from the exodus of the Israelites out of Egypt through the occupation of the promised land. During this period, Moses used miracles to deliver and sustain God's chosen people (Exodus 4:1-17).

2. The Prophetic period, which includes the ministries of Elijah, Elisha, and Isaiah, who used miracles to deliver the Israelites from idolatry (1 Kings 18).

3. The Apostolic period, from the time of Jesus to the ministries of the apostles and the establishment of

> the first-century church to validate the new way
> God was saving his people from sin (Hebrews 2:1-4).

Almost all the miracles recorded in the Bible—with the obvious exception of the creation of the world at the beginning and the return of Christ at the end—take place during these three clusters. And once the church was established at the end of the third cluster, the miracles ceased. But why would that be the case? The cessationists have an answer.

"God never changes, but his program on earth does" is the common argument given for the cessation of miracles. "There are different stages of his redemptive plan," writes Norman Geisler, "and what is true in one stage is untrue in another."[4] During these three periods of history, God used miracles to reveal himself so people could know his true character and power. But there is no longer a need for God to reveal himself miraculously because everything we need to know about God is now contained in his holy Word, the Bible.

"The Bible we have is more than even the first-century Christians possessed," writes Geisler. "It is complete and sufficient for faith and practice. Pentecost does not need to be repeated any more than Calvary and the empty tomb."[5]

According to the cessationists, through these three periods—the Mosaic, the Prophetic, and the Apostolic—God used miracles to show his greatness, glory, and saving power. Today he accomplishes these things in other ways. We can see his greatness through the created world, and the more science discovers about the wonders of the creation, the more we see the glory of God through all he has made. As for God's deliverance, the power of the gospel is all we need to confirm God's saving power over sin and suffering.

Whether or not you have ever heard these reasons for why

miracles have stopped, you have been influenced by them. I certainly was. None of my pastors ever preached that miracles no longer occur because the Bible is "complete and sufficient for faith and practice," but they didn't need to. In the conservative evangelical churches I have attended throughout my life, the Bible was all my pastors taught.

I now realize I have been missing out.

What I am about to share with you should not detract from the Bible's place and position as the authoritative, inspired, inerrant Word of God. Throughout my Christian life I have read and studied the Bible with the goal of becoming someone who "correctly explains the word of truth" (2 Timothy 2:15). I fully believe the Bible is essential for faith and practice. But is the Bible all we need to follow Jesus and live the way he wants us to? I have come to believe that it is not, if by sufficient we mean there is no other way God speaks to us today.

I Was a Bible Deist

Remember our brief discussion in chapter 1 about deism? Deists believe in God, but they believe he created the world and then withdrew from all he made, leaving us to run things using human reason and know-how. Following this definition, I want to introduce you to a concept known as Bible deism.

I first became aware of Bible deism while reading a book by Dallas Willard called *Hearing God.* Here is Willard's terse definition: "Bible deism holds that God gave us the Bible and then went away." Willard compares Bible deism to a belief held by the Sadducees during the time of Jesus. They taught that God stopped speaking when he finished speaking with Moses, so anything or anyone who claimed to speak for God was invalid.

According to Willard, Bible deists believe that God stopped speaking when the Bible was finished, "leaving us to make what we could of it, with no individual communication either through the Bible or otherwise."[6]

To the Bible deist, "sufficiency of Scripture" means that the only way God speaks today is through the Bible. In his book *Surprised by the Voice of God,* Jack Deere talks about three unsettling implications of this belief.[7] First, it's possible to have a relationship with a book rather than a person. I know, that sounds harsh, but think about it. Isn't it easier to relate to a "system of interpretive rules and a set of traditions" than it is to relate to a person we've never actually met, you know, *in person*?

The second unsettling implication is that the Bible deist depends on his or her own *interpretation* of Scripture rather than on Scripture itself. You and I may both agree that Scripture is sufficient for faith and practice, but what if we disagree on what the Bible means in a particular case? Whose interpretation of a Bible passage is sufficient, yours or mine?

The third and probably most unsettling implication of Bible deism is that it puts us in control. If God only speaks through the Bible, then it is my job to know the Bible so well that I know what to do in every situation. There's little or no room for God to speak to me and tell me what to do outside the pages of Scripture.

This was me. I didn't call myself a Bible deist, but for all practical purposes, all three of these implications were true of me because I lived my life as if God wrote the Bible and then went away. Thankfully, in the process of writing this book, God has revealed the flaws in the way I was looking at the Bible.

First, I have come to recognize that when I trusted Jesus by faith for my salvation, the Bible was not enough. Even reading

John 3:16 was not enough. The Holy Spirit had to convict me of my need for a Savior and turn my heart to Jesus. Jack Deere puts it this way:

> In principle, we acknowledge that we would never have become Christians apart from the supernatural revelatory ministry of the Holy Spirit. But now that we are "in," we seem to think that we progress through intelligence rather than through the revelatory ministry of the Holy Spirit.[8]

Second, I realize now that I was reading and studying the Bible as a book of doctrine and abstract truth about knowing God and living the Christian life. It's painful to admit this to you, but my relationship with the Bible was probably stronger than my relationship with Jesus.

Third, the way I was reading and interpreting the Bible had a bias against the supernatural. On a practical level I had bought into cessationist thinking, and it caused me to come to a conclusion that startles me now. I believed that the extraordinary experiences of the characters in the Bible were true, but I didn't believe they could happen today, especially to me or anyone I know.

Dallas Willard writes that believing the Bible stories means much more than believing they happened to people in the Bible.

> Conversely, if we are really to understand the Bible record, we must enter into our study of it on the assumption that the experiences recorded there are basically of the same type ours would have been if we had been there...Unless this comes home to us, the things that happened to the people in the Bible will remain unreal to us.[9]

According to Willard, this failure to believe that the accounts of miracles and healings in the Bible could happen to us today is the reason people stop reading the Bible. Or if they read it at all, they do not experience any excitement or joy. "In my opinion, based on considerable experience," Willard continues, "this is primarily because they do not know and are not taught how to understand the experience of biblical characters in terms of how they experience life."[10]

I Was Embarrassed by the Supernatural

I have been to just one healing service, and I was embarrassed, not just for myself but for the people in the service. The preacher, who wasn't really a faith healer as such, was charismatic in both senses of the word. His sparkling smile, powerful speaking voice, and well-tailored suit combined to give him *charisma.* And he was *charismatic* in that he exhibited several outward "manifestations" of the Spirit, including prophetic utterances, speaking in tongues, and healing. I don't recall if anyone was healed that night, but there was plenty of shouting and ecstatic utterances from the audience. A few people swayed and swooned, and the preacher was at the center of it all.

It was as if I were in a movie with characters directly from charismatic central casting. It was a surreal experience, at least for me. Most others in the audience, including the person who brought me to the service, seemed to be immersed in the experience.

My intention is not to paint a negative or even a stereotypical picture of churches and preachers with a healing ministry. I'm sharing this story to illustrate the embarrassment and uneasiness many mainline and conservative Christians feel about people steeped in charismatic or Pentecostal signs and wonders, especially healing. If you've never been to a healing service, perhaps you have watched one on television or YouTube. You've seen the excesses, and it probably embarrassed you just the same.

Some healing ministries like the one I witnessed are part of the broader prosperity gospel movement. Loosely defined, the prosperity gospel sends a message that God wants every one of his faithful followers to enjoy perfect health and financial security. The proponents of this philosophy use Scripture to justify their claims, but the verses they cite are usually taken out of context. More seriously, the intent of the prosperity gospel—perfect health and worldly riches—runs contrary to the life of Jesus, something we will look at more closely in the next chapter.

Yes, healing is in the Bible, but it's not found in a celestial vending machine or divine jukebox. God doesn't dance just because we put a coin in the slot, yet some believe that if you have enough faith to say the right words, God is obligated to do what you expect. "A false god might promise to deliver everything you want," writes Eugene Peterson. "The one true God promises to always meet your needs. If you seek to gain everything you want, you'll be disappointed in him."[11]

So most of us, embarrassed by this attempted manipulation of the supernatural, run the other way and become wholly practical and natural. For all intents and purposes, we become Bible deists.

At the same time, if we're being completely honest with each other here, let's admit something. We may think we're not caught up in the prosperity gospel movement, but don't we all want God to cure our illnesses and help us financially? We may criticize the health-and-wealth gospel, but when we're sick or when a loved one has cancer, we pray for physical healing. And when things aren't going well financially, we pray for wealth.

We all ask God to give us what we want most, but rather than praying for God to do something miraculous, we just use more practical language. We want the doctors to heal our sick loved one, and we want God to provide that new job we desperately need. We just aren't inclined to ask God for a miracle, mainly because we don't really expect miracles to happen.

CAN WE BELIEVE IN MIRACLES AND HEALING?

At the beginning of this book I stated that I have never personally experienced a miracle, and I have never seen a healing. Jack Deere is convinced that my story is typical of most Christians. We do not disbelieve because we are biased against the supernatural, or embarrassed by the supernatural, or even afraid of being disappointed in the supernatural. Rather, we don't believe miracles can happen today because we have not personally experienced them.

And yet there is something about miracles and healing that continue to draw us in. We may never have experienced a miracle like those in the Bible, but we wonder what that would be like. We may have settled for a practical doctrine-only Christian experience where the emphasis is on our inner lives, but we wonder what it would be like for God to interrupt our natural world with supernatural signs and wonders. We may dismiss and even ridicule the faith healers who seem to manipulate people, but there's something about the connection they try to make with God on an outward physical level that makes us wonder, *What if this would happen to me or someone I love?*

CHAPTER 3

The Three Greatest Miracles

If you grew up in the church as I did, there are certain miracles in the Bible you remember because they made for great adventure stories. The characters involved were bigger than life, and the miracles opened your imagination. The stories with larger-than-life characters made the biggest impression on my grade-school self, so my top three had to be Moses, Samson, and Jonah.

Moses is at the top of my list because of the sheer quantity and drama of his miraculous exploits. Of course, my admiration was aided by *The Ten Commandments*, the movie directed by Cecil B. DeMille, starring Charlton Heston. As a kid I recall watching with amazement as Hollywood magic depicted the various miracles Charlton, I mean Moses, performed with the mere tap of his six-foot staff. The parting of the Red Sea, when Pharaoh (played by the intense Yul Brenner) watched in horror as his men and their horses drowned beneath the crashing waves after the Israelites walked safely to the other side, both shocked and delighted me. The good guys won at last!

Next on my list was Samson, and what's not to like about this Old Testament long-haired character, who served God as a judge (albeit a rather poor one). When I first heard the story of Samson, what with his superhuman feats of strength and the final act of bringing down the temple of the Philistine god Dagon, I was enthralled. Superman had nothing on Samson.

And then there was Jonah and his three-day experience in the belly of the whale. That story looked especially cool on the flannel-graph board (I know, I'm dating myself). Like every other kid in my third-grade Sunday school class, I stared open-mouthed as the teacher explained how God took care of Jonah, and wouldn't he do the same thing for us?

There are many other miracles recorded in the Bible—101 in the Old Testament and 130 more in the New Testament, including 52 miracles performed by or involving Jesus. That number alone astounds me. I feel stressed when my calendar fills up with conference calls, meetings, and projects. It's hard to fathom the intense pressure Jesus must have felt as the crowds crushed into him, many sick or deformed or possessed by demons, desperate to feel the healing touch of the man from Galilee.

> When they came down from the mountain, the disciples stood with Jesus on a large, level area, surrounded by many of his followers and by the crowds. There were people from all over Judea and from Jerusalem and from as far north as the seacoasts of Tyre and Sidon. They had come to hear him and to be healed of their diseases; and those troubled by evil spirits were healed. Everyone tried to touch him, because healing power went out from him, and he healed everyone (Luke 6:17-19).

WHY SO MANY MIRACLES?

A miracle occurs when God or someone who speaks for God does something supernatural. Sometimes a miracle verifies that the one doing the miracle is truly speaking for God. Other times a miracle proves that God is, well, God. When he confronted the prophets of Baal, Elijah asked God directly for a miracle for both of these reasons. "O LORD, God of Abraham, Isaac, and Jacob," he prayed, "prove today that you are God in Israel and that I am your servant. Prove that I have done all this at your command" (1 Kings 18:36).

Even Jesus was both confirmed and revealed by the miracles he performed. We already looked at Jesus' first miracle, turning water into wine at the wedding in Cana, which convinced the disciples that Jesus was genuinely sent by God. Three years later, after the crucifixion and resurrection of Jesus, the apostle John summarized the purpose of the many miracles Jesus performed:

> The disciples saw Jesus do many other miraculous signs in addition to the ones recorded in this book. But these are written so that you may continue to believe that Jesus is the Messiah, the Son of God, and that by believing in him you will have life by the power of his name (John 20:30-31).

A few days later, just before Jesus ascended into heaven, he gave his followers (called *apostles* because they were about to be "sent out" to tell the world about the resurrected Christ) these instructions:

> "You will receive power when the Holy Spirit comes upon you. And you will be my witnesses, telling people about me everywhere—in Jerusalem,

throughout Judea, in Samaria, and to the ends of the earth" (Acts 1:8).

The miracles performed by the apostles following the ascension of Jesus, mostly recorded in the book of Acts, gave them credibility. Here is what Paul wrote to the church in Corinth:

> When I was with you, I certainly gave you proof that I am an apostle. For I patiently did many signs and wonders and miracles among you (2 Corinthians 12:12).

From these examples in the Old and New Testaments, we can come to an understanding of *the purposes of miracles in the Bible*:

- to glorify the nature of God

  > This miraculous sign at Cana in Galilee was the first time Jesus revealed his glory. And his disciples believed in him (John 2:11).

- to credential certain people to speak for God

  > God confirmed the message by giving signs and wonders and various miracles and gifts of the Holy Spirit whenever he chose (Hebrews 2:4).

- to provide evidence for belief in God and his Son, Jesus

  > A huge crowd kept following him wherever he went, because they saw his miraculous signs as he healed the sick (John 6:2).

Each of the 231 miracles recorded in the Bible is significant. But rather than list and explain each one, I'd like to share with you what I believe are the three greatest miracles in the Bible. These miracles provide a big-picture view of the greatness and power and love of almighty God. In a sense, every other miracle in the Bible flows from these three.

THE GREAT MIRACLE: CREATION

In his excellent book *The Case for Miracles,* Lee Strobel calls the creation of the universe the "granddaddy of all miracles."[1] I won't argue with that. If God had not brought the material, natural world into existence, we wouldn't be here talking about miracles and healing. In fact, we wouldn't be here at all.

My purpose here is not to *prove* to you that God created the universe. That's the subject for another book. In fact, Bruce Bickel and I wrote *Creation and Evolution 101* in 2004 to give straightforward and easy-to-understand answers to questions about how the universe came into existence.[2] What I want to show here is why the creation of the universe is the greatest miracle of all.

In the Beginning

The first three words in the Bible set the stage for the miracle of creation. You may accept the view that God created the universe six thousand to ten thousand years ago in a period of six literal twenty-four-hour days (called young earth creationism). Or you may believe that God created the universe ten to fifteen billion years ago over a longer period than six literal days (called old earth creationism). Or you may embrace theistic evolution, a view that points to natural selection as God's way of creating and populating the world with living things. What you believe about *when* or *how* God created the world is immaterial. The real issue is not *when* or *how* but *who*. The real issue is God.

What is the miracle of creation? Hebrews 11:3 explains it simply but elegantly: "By faith we understand that the entire universe was formed at God's command, that what we now see did not come from anything that can be seen."

From this verse we learn two things about the miracle of creation. First, God *spoke* the universe into existence. Second, he created the vast material universe out of nothing. Honestly, even though I believe this miracle, I have to think deeper about how God could pull this off. There has to be a logical explanation for the great miracle of creation.

Because the Bible isn't a scientific book, you won't find detailed scientific explanations for how the universe came into existence. What you will find, however, are descriptions of the qualities God possesses that "qualify" him to be the creator.

For example, anything that exists—whether it's the chair you sit in or the world you live in—must have a cause. And because it's logically impossible for there to be an infinite number of causes, there must be a first cause, something that got the first thing—in this case the universe—going. God is the only being capable and qualified to be a first cause because he is the only being who was not caused. This fits with who God is. God is self-existent and he has always existed, which means he existed *before* the beginning and is the first cause of every created material thing: Supernatural God creating the natural universe.

God Is Qualified

Here are some other qualities God possesses that qualify him to be the creator of the world. He is:

Transcendent. If God created the universe, then he could not have been part of it. When we say God is independent of the universe, we mean that God is *transcendent.* Here is what he says about himself:

> "My thoughts are nothing like your thoughts," says
> the LORD.
> > "And my ways are far beyond anything you
> > could imagine.
> For just as the heavens are higher than the earth,
> > so my ways are higher than your ways
> > and my thoughts higher than your thoughts."
> > > > (Isaiah 55:8-9)

Omnipotent. The power and energy required to bring the universe into existence is unfathomable. Only an *omnipotent* (all-powerful) God would possess that much power. The prophet Jeremiah observes,

> O Sovereign LORD! You made the heavens and earth
> by your strong hand and powerful arm. Nothing is
> too hard for you! (Jeremiah 32:17).

Eternal and infinite. In order to create the universe out of nothing, God had to exist before time and matter began. That's a perfect description of God. He is *eternal* in relationship to matter and *infinite* in relationship to time. God says about himself:

> "I am the Alpha and the Omega—the beginning and
> the end," says the Lord God. "I am the one who
> is, who always was, and who is still to come—the
> Almighty One" (Revelation 1:8).

Omniscient. Only an *omniscient* (all-knowing) God would know how to set the universe in motion with all the properties and physical laws that allow it to operate with such precision and beauty. The psalmist writes,

> How great is our Lord! His power is absolute!
> His understanding is beyond comprehension!
> (Psalm 147:5)

The more we learn about how the universe functions, the more the evidence points to a self-existent, transcendent, supremely powerful, eternal, infinitely wise personal *being*, rather than some abstract force or power, who created the universe. In their book *The Privileged Planet*, Guillermo Gonzalez and Jay Richards ask:

> Is it possible that this immense, symphonic system of atoms, fields, forces, stars, galaxies, and people is the result of a choice, a purpose or intention, rather than simply some inscrutable outworking of blind necessity or an inexplicable accident?[3]

That is the great miracle of creation.

THE GRAND MIRACLE: THE INCARNATION

There is a direct connection between the *great* miracle—creation—and the *grand* miracle—the incarnation. The connection is, strangely enough, a little word with big implications: sin.

God's creation was perfect. The supernatural and natural lived in beautiful, perfect harmony, immaterial God interacting with material humans without any need for an intermediary. God walked with his human creation in the cool of the day.

Because God created humanity with the ability to choose or reject him, to obey or disobey him (it's called free will), God opened up the possibility for sin to enter the world (sin simply means to fall short of God's perfect standard). And so it did, breaking the harmony of an unblemished relationship between supernatural God and his natural creation. Adam and Eve, our biological and spiritual parents, were banished from the garden to a life of toil, strife, and hardship. They were in a bad way, and all of their descendants would inherit the sting of their punishment: separation from the supernatural God who made them and the possibility that they would die.

Only it wasn't the end. Adam and Eve may have been helpless, but they were not without hope. Even as God was pronouncing the fate of Satan, the snake who deceived our first parents, he provided a preview of the coming Savior who would defeat the enemy and make things right, though not without a price:

> "And I will cause hostility between you and the
> woman,
>   and between your offspring and her offspring.
> He will strike your head,
>   and you will strike his heel."
>   (Genesis 3:15)

This is the first prophecy out of more than forty in the Old Testament concerning Jesus, God's only Son, born of a woman, God himself in human form, sent to earth to deliver humankind from the grip and consequence of sin, thereby restoring the relationship between supernatural God and his human creation. This is what the incarnation is all about.

I want to step back for a moment to consider the significance of the incarnation—the act of an all-powerful, all-knowing, all-everything God taking on the form of a human being. *Incarnation* simply means "in the flesh." That's who Jesus is. God in the flesh. The apostle Paul describes Jesus in a grand poetic way. Notice how the qualities of Christ align perfectly with the qualities of God we talked about in the great miracle:

> Christ is the visible image of the invisible God.
>> He existed before anything was created and is
>> supreme over all creation,
> for through him God created everything
>> in the heavenly realms and on earth.
> He made the things we can see
>> and the things we can't see—
> such as thrones, kingdoms, rulers, and authorities
> in the unseen world.
>> Everything was created through him and for him.
> He existed before anything else,
>> and he holds all creation together.
> Christ is also the head of the church,
>> which is his body.
> He is the beginning,
>> supreme over all who rise from the dead.
>> So he is first in everything.
> For God in all his fullness
>> was pleased to live in Christ,
> and through him God reconciled
>> everything to himself.
> He made peace with everything in heaven and on
> earth
>> by means of Christ's blood on the cross.
>
> (Colossians 1:15-20)

C.S. Lewis has this to say about the grand miracle:

> The central miracle asserted by Christians is the Incarnation. They say that God became Man. Every other miracle prepares for this, or exhibits this, or results from this. Just as every natural event is the manifestation at a particular place and moment of Nature's total character, so every particular Christian miracle manifests at a particular place and moment the character and significance of the Incarnation.[4]

And in *Surprised by the Power of the Spirit*, Jack Deere writes,

> The most amazing supernatural event ever to occur was the incarnation and then the death of the eternal Son in the place of sinful humanity, followed by his bodily resurrection. Surely the greatest wonder is that by faith alone in Jesus Christ we receive the gift of eternal life. Surely the greatest power any human will ever know is the power of the cross of Jesus Christ. Through the cross we not only have forgiveness but also access into God's glorious presence.[5]

The Miracles of Jesus

Craig Keener is widely considered the foremost contemporary biblical scholar on miracles. Many consider his two-volume set, *Miracles: The Credibility of the New Testament Accounts*, the most comprehensive and best researched book on the topic. Lee Strobel asked Keener a question that goes to the heart of the grand miracle: "Why did Jesus heal the sick, boss around nature, and cast out demons?"[6] Keener's reply is the best explanation I have seen:

His miracles were a sign of the inbreaking of the kingdom—or rule—of God. They were a taste of the future where healing will be complete. Jesus said, "But if I drive out demons by the finger of God, then the kingdom of God has come upon you" (Luke 11:20). These signs were a prelude to the entire restoration, when God will make a new heaven and a new earth. They remind us that a day is coming when there will be no more suffering or pain.[7]

The stories of the miracles of Jesus, including his many healings, are recorded in the four Gospels, or biographies, of Jesus. Between these four eyewitness accounts, there are fifty-two miracles attributed to Jesus, including his resurrection and post-resurrection appearances in his glorified body. I decided to focus on the book of Mark, the shortest of the four Gospels, to get a sense of how many miracles Jesus performed in each category—healing people, casting out demons, and showing power over nature.

There are eleven stories in Mark about Jesus healing people, six instances where Jesus cast out demons, six stories about Jesus demonstrating power over nature, and two times when there was a resurrection—including his own. In reading these miracles one by one, I was impressed with three things.

First, the healings were not accompanied by any big fanfare. Jesus healed as if it were a natural part of his supernatural life.

Second, the miracles show Jesus' compassion as well as his power. In fact, compassion seems to be the motivation for healing. Several times Jesus was "moved with compassion," whether he was healing someone or feeding thousands of hungry people.

The third and perhaps most moving thing I noticed is that when Jesus healed, he usually touched the person who was crippled, deaf, or blind. So powerful and meaningful was the touch of Jesus that in one account, "all who touched him were healed," even if they simply touched the fringe of his robe (Mark 6:56). When the supernatural touches the natural in that liminal space where heaven and earth meet, it isn't some cold, objective experience. When we encounter God in this way, we can feel his touch. We experience his compassion and grace. Even more, we get a foretaste of the time when God will bring an end to suffering and defeat death once and for all.

The Resurrection of Jesus

The miracle of the resurrection of Jesus Christ is absolutely essential to the Christian story. Without the resurrection, the incarnation loses its strength. If Jesus did not come back from the dead, in effect God is dead and all who put their faith in Jesus are no better off than they were before. Paul doesn't hold back when he considers this possibility:

> And if Christ has not been raised, then your faith
> is useless and you are still guilty of your sins. In
> that case, all who have died believing in Christ are
> lost! And if our hope in Christ is only for this life,
> we are more to be pitied than anyone in the world
> (1 Corinthians 15:17-18).

Through the centuries since the resurrection, scholars and skeptics alike have done their best to mount arguments against the resurrection of Jesus. In fact, it started on that first Easter morning. When religious leaders who called for the execution of Jesus realized he was no longer in the tomb, they paid the guards to fabricate a story about the disciples of Jesus coming in the night to take his body (Matthew 28:11-15). However, the conspiracy theory lost all credibility when Jesus appeared to his disciples and then to more than five hundred of his followers, and finally to Paul himself (1 Corinthians 15:4-8; Acts 9:1-6). Paul knew the resurrection was not a myth or a made-up story. It was absolutely, unequivocally true:

> But in fact, Christ has been raised from the dead.
> He is the first of a great harvest of all who have died
> (1 Corinthians 15:20).

Let's camp on that phrase for a moment: "He is the first of a great harvest of all who have died." I like how Eugene Peterson phrases it in The Message: "the first in a long legacy of those who are going to leave the cemeteries." The incarnation was fulfilled in the resurrection, which now sets up the third great miracle.

THE COMING MIRACLE: RESTORATION

There are more than forty miracles in Revelation, the last book of the Bible. All of these concern events that haven't yet happened. These miracles are visions of the future, given to the apostle John, who wrote the Gospel of John and three letters that bear his name. Revelation is difficult to understand, leading to a variety of interpretations as to when these events will take place. Maybe that's why pastors tend to stay away from this book, choosing instead to preach on practical matters of faith and practice.

There was a time when you would routinely hear messages on Revelation and Bible prophecy in church. Maybe too many messages, leading many of the faithful to obsess about Bible prophecy and future events at the expense of caring too little about the present world. Now it seems the pendulum has swung too far the other way, to the point that Christians today care too little about the world to come.

Truth is, we need to focus on both the present world and also the world to come. As Christians, we are *already* the beneficiaries of God's redemption plan, which he made possible through the life, death, and resurrection of Jesus. At the same time, we need to keep this present life in perspective, knowing that the natural, material world we inhabit is but a foretaste of the world *not yet* here.

From Creation to Completion

The great miracle of creation, the grand miracle of the incarnation, and the coming miracle of restoration all proceed from God, but all three persons in the Godhead—Father, Son, and Hoy Spirit—are involved in this supernatural drama from creation to completion.

At the same time, God has chosen to make Jesus the centerpiece of the drama of human history. As Bruce and I state in our book, *Knowing God 101*:

- Jesus is the Source of all creation (John 1:1-3).
- Jesus is the Sustainer of all creation (Colossians 1:17).
- Jesus is the Redeemer of sinful humanity (Ephesians 1:7).
- Jesus is the Resolution of God's plan for human history (1 Corinthians 15:24).[8]

Appropriately, the fantastical visions given to John in the book of Revelation begin with a vision of Jesus:

When I saw him, I fell at his feet as if I were dead.
But he laid his right hand on me and said, "Don't
be afraid! I am the First and the Last. I am the living
one. I died, but look—I am alive forever and ever!
And I hold the keys of death and the grave" (Revelation 1:17-18).

How Will the Coming Miracle Unfold?

Just as people disagree on when and how the great miracle of creation unfolded, there are several views on when and
how the coming miracle of restoration will unfold. And just as
the real issue of creation is God, the real issue of completion
is Christ.

There's nothing wrong with trying to speculate on the
sequence and timing of the miraculous events that will take place
in the future. It's in our nature to want to know what's coming.
Two thousand years ago the disciples of Jesus were curious about
the future, so they asked him: "Tell us, when will all this happen? What sign will signal your return and the end of the world?"
(Matthew 24:3).

The extensive reply Jesus gave in what is known as the Olivet
Discourse (because he taught these things while sitting on the
slopes of the Mount of Olives) is filled with warnings, advice,
parables, and some direct instructions about the fates of the
unjust and the righteous. From the words of Jesus, we can be sure
that the coming miracle will include these events:

- the coming of Jesus Christ "on the clouds of heaven
  with power and great glory" (Matthew 24:30)

- a future bodily resurrection when the dead will

stand before God at his appointed time (Matthew 25:31-32)

- final judgment for all people, with the result that those who followed Christ will go into eternal life and those who refused Christ will go away into eternal punishment (Matthew 25:33-46)

The miraculous coming of Jesus Christ is hard to wrap our minds around, but we shouldn't let the fantastic nature of the miracles associated with these end-time events keep us from accepting them as nothing less than absolute reality. These things will happen, even if we don't know how or when. If we have any doubts, we need only go to the writings of the apostle Paul, who painted a spectacular word picture that came to him "directly from the Lord":

> We who are still living when the Lord returns will not meet him ahead of those who have died. For the Lord himself will come down from heaven with a commanding shout, with the voice of the archangel, and with the trumpet call of God. First, the believers who have died will rise from their graves. Then, together with them, we who are still alive and remain on the earth will be caught up in the clouds to meet the Lord in the air. Then we will be with the Lord forever. So encourage each other with these words (1 Thessalonians 4:15-18).

We Will Be with the Lord Forever

The coming of the Lord at some future time is but the prelude to the most unimaginable yet completely real existence for all who have been transformed by the incarnate Christ, whose life, death, resurrection, and ascension made it possible for us to be restored into a seamless, unbroken, intimate relationship with our creator God.

This is the return to Eden, that perfect place of unblemished beauty where God and humankind lived together in perfect harmony. Once again the supernatural and natural will dwell together, only it will be forever. Through the miracles of God throughout human history, we have caught glimpses of Eden. Someday we will live in Eden again, only it will be infinitely better. We will experience the miracle of a new heaven and a new earth.

Near the end of Revelation, John sees the vision that gives hope to humanity. This is what Craig Keener referred to when he said the miracles of Jesus were a taste of the future where our healing will be complete.

> Then I saw a new heaven and a new earth, for the old heaven and the old earth had disappeared. And the sea was also gone. And I saw the holy city, the new Jerusalem, coming down from God out of heaven like a bride beautifully dressed for her husband.
>
> I heard a loud shout from the throne, saying, "Look, God's home is now among his people! He will live with them, and they will be his people. God himself will be with them. He will wipe every tear from their eyes, and there will be no more death or sorrow or crying or pain. All these things are gone forever."
>
> And the one sitting on the throne said, "Look, I am making everything new!" And then he said to me, "Write this down, for what I tell you is trustworthy and true." And he also said, "It is finished! I

am the Alpha and the Omega—the Beginning and
the End. To all who are thirsty I will give freely from
the springs of the water of life" (Revelation 21:1-6).

According to Keener, the miracles we read about in the Bible,
in particular the miracles of Jesus, were "a sign of the inbreaking
of the kingdom—or the rule—of God." They were a preview of
a glorious future when "healing will be complete."[9] As difficult
as it has been to trace the story of my father's journey from life
to death, I have total confidence that he is already experiencing a
foretaste of the total restoration of heaven and earth yet to come
for all who trust in Jesus for their salvation. As soon as he passed
from this life on earth to his life in the presence of Jesus, he was
completely healed. I take great comfort in that reality.

Thinking about the three greatest miracles, along with the
other 231 individual miracles recorded in the pages of Scripture,
makes me wonder about miracles and healing today. Do they
offer the same glimpses of God's coming miracle of restoration?
How do we know they are real? We will explore these questions
in the next chapter.

CHAPTER 4

Healing and Miracles Today

M y uncle Sam, my father's brother, the one who took him to A.W. Tozer's house so Tozer could pray for my father's healing, went on to become a leader in the Christian and Missionary Alliance Church. He was a professor in one of its seminaries and even served as the general editor of the denominational magazine, *The Alliance Weekly*, a position Tozer once held. As a church leader, Sam had the opportunity to observe trends in the global church, mostly by reviewing thousands of reports submitted by missionaries around the world.

Through the years he received dramatic accounts of miraculous healings, especially from those areas of "new work with new believers." From these reports, Sam noticed a pattern. As the work matured, the healings diminished. Sam would quote Mark 16:17-18, where Jesus says, "These miraculous signs will accompany those who believe...They will be able to place their hands on the sick, and they will be healed." Sam wondered: *Do new believers have a fresh, untarnished, and simple faith that isn't compromised by experience?*

There is no shortage of authenticated accounts of healing in the world today. Following the publication of his respected book

Miracles: The Credibility of the New Testament Account, Craig Keener continues to report healings from around the world, particularly in the Global South. In an article titled "Real Raisings from the Dead or Fake News?" published in *Christianity Today*, Keener shares some startling stories of current-day healings, and yes, even resurrections.

Keener's own wife, Medine, who was raised in the Republic of Congo, recounts the healing of her two-year old sister, Therese, after she was bitten by a snake. The little girl seemed to have stopped breathing, and since no medical attention was available in their village, Medine's mother strapped Therese to her back and ran to a neighboring village for help.

By the time they arrived three hours later, Therese was likely "either brain dead or had sustained significant brain damage." An evangelist in a nearby village was summoned. He and Medine's mother "prayed over the lifeless girl and immediately she started breathing again." By the next day she was fine, with no apparent brain damage. "Therese has a master's degree and is a pastor in Congo," writes Keener.[1]

It's tempting to read stories like this and conclude that they could never happen to us, mainly because the stories always seem to come from other places, especially Africa and Asia. Keener agrees that miracles and healings like the one experienced by his sister-in-law seem to occur with frequency in countries outside the U.S. "Some estimate that 90 percent of the growth of the church in China is being fueled by healings," Keener said.[2]

"In America, we have a lot of sophisticated medical technology, which is God's gift to us, and we should use it," Keener continued. "That's the way he typically brings healings. But in many other places around the world, that's not available, and perhaps God's intervention is the only hope in a lot of instances."[3]

WHY NOT HERE? WHY NOT NOW?

There's no questioning Strobel's research or Keener's credibility, but I will admit to you that I am left a little flat when I read about spectacular miracles in other countries. As convincing and real as the stories told by Strobel and Keener and many others are, I have yet to personally experience a healing miracle. Nor has anyone I prayed for been healed, at least not the kind of instantaneous way we read about in the Bible or in books like *The Case for Miracles*. But that doesn't mean I don't believe it *could* happen.

I suspect you have also prayed for healing more than once—for yourself, for a family member, or for a friend. Like me, you are convinced God *can* heal, and you believe he *wants* to heal, but you are not completely certain God *will* heal.

Why do we struggle to believe God will heal when we ask him? I have thought about this question for a long time. Perhaps my background, knowing that God didn't heal my father, and then growing up in a certain kind of church tradition—where healing was never talked about, let alone experienced—has tilted my belief away from believing in miraculous healing for today. Maybe I still have a bias against the supernatural—not because I don't believe God *can* heal, but because I'm not completely convinced God *will* heal.

As I have become more aware of this bias, I have begun to make conscious, deliberate efforts to become more open to the supernatural—and not just the practical—Christian life. Even more, I find myself wanting to *live* the supernatural life I have been given. And that includes living in the reality of the healing power of God—not just in the Bible, but right now. I want to live this way because I know people who are sick, I know people who are living with chronic pain, and I know people who are dying. I want more than anything for them to be well, and I don't see any other way for that to happen than for God to heal them.

If you want to live in that reality as well, follow me on a journey to discover *why* God heals. As we look at these reasons, pulled from the pages of Scripture, we will gain confidence that God heals today as he always has.

WHY GOD HEALS

When you read the stories of healing in the Bible, certain patterns emerge that help us to understand why God heals. As I have searched the Scriptures and read as many books on healing as I can get my hands on, I have noticed three reasons why God heals. These are by no means exhaustive, but they have helped me form some context for healing today.[4] God doesn't change, so perhaps his reasons for healing in the Bible will help us see more clearly why God heals today.

God Heals to Show His Power and Grace

For this first reason, I want to start pretty early in the Bible, in the book of Exodus, where God first proclaims, "I am the LORD who heals you" (15:26). The story of the exodus is well known. The Israelites escape from their captivity in Egypt after God miraculously brings the ten plagues to Pharaoh, who relents and lets God's people go. God then leads them to the Red Sea with the Egyptians in hot pursuit. Just when it looks as if the Israelites will be captured again, God parts the Red Sea so the entire nation can cross on dry ground. Behind them, the water engulfs the pursuing army, causing Miriam, the sister of Moses and Aaron, to rejoice with this song:

> "Sing to the LORD,
>   for he is highly exalted.
> Both horse and driver
>   he has hurled into the sea."
>
> (Exodus 15:21 NIV)

In the very next scene, Moses has been leading Israel from the Red Sea into the desert. For three days they travel without finding water. When they finally come to Marah, they find water, but it is not fit to drink because it is bitter. The people complain against Moses, saying, "What are we to drink?" Here's what Moses does next.

> So Moses cried out to the LORD for help, and the LORD showed him a piece of wood. Moses threw it into the water, and this made the water good to drink (Exodus 15:25).

Most translations of this verse are like the one you just read. They say Moses grabbed *a piece of wood*. However, the Hebrew word here is more like *a tree*. God then tells Moses to cast the *tree* into the bitter water, which makes it good to drink. I like this translation of the word because of what it represents. "The tree cast into the waters at Marah may be taken as a symbol of the cross of Christ, which in turn symbolizes God's ultimate healing power," writes Elmer Towns.[5]

Indeed, this is the first time in Scripture where God gives himself the title *Jehovah Rophe*, a name that means "to restore, heal, or cure." It also has the meaning of a physician in both a physical and spiritual sense. God puts it simply: "I am the LORD who heals you" (Exodus 15:26).

Throughout the Old Testament, we see the various ways God heals:

Physically

> Let all that I am praise the LORD;
>> may I never forget the good things he does for me.
>
> He forgives all my sins
>> and heals all my diseases.
>
>> (Psalm 103:2-3)

Emotionally

> He heals the brokenhearted
>> and bandages their wounds.
>
>> (Psalm 147:3)

Spiritually

> But he was pierced for our rebellion,
>> crushed for our sins.
>
> He was beaten so we could be whole.
>> He was whipped so we could be healed.
>>> (Isaiah 53:5)

God makes it clear, both in his words and his actions, that he has the power to heal us in every dimension of life.

God Heals Out of Compassion and Mercy

The verse from Isaiah 53 is a prophecy concerning the coming Messiah, Jesus Christ. God's ultimate plan to heal broken people—to turn their bitter water into water fit to drink—is fully realized in the person and work of his one and only Son. The tree that Moses drops into the water at God's command symbolizes the cross upon which Jesus died. He had to taste the bitter water; Jesus was crushed for our sins; and he was whipped so we could be healed.

Jesus did all of this out of his deep love and compassion for us, and it is from his *compassion*—which means to "suffer with"—that he heals us physically, emotionally, and spiritually. The prophet Jeremiah penned one of the most beautiful poetic lines in all of literature, describing the compassion of God:

> Because of the LORD's great love we are not consumed,
>> for his compassions never fail.
> They are new every morning;
>> great is your faithfulness.
>>>> (Lamentations 3:22-23 NIV)

Far from being a dispassionate God who doesn't care about us, God understands our weaknesses and desires to bring us healing and hope. Love motivates God's compassion, and Jesus demonstrates it in a most personal way.

Jehovah Rophe has the meaning of "physician," and that title is realized fully in Jesus. When the Pharisees criticized him for eating with tax collectors and sinners, Jesus said to them, "Healthy people don't need a doctor—sick people do. I have come to call not those who think they are righteous, but those who know they are sinners" (Mark 2:17). Of course, Jesus came to save sinners. He suffered with us and for us, willingly giving his life so that all who believe in him can have eternal life (John 3:16).

But Jesus also came to bring hope and healing to those who are suffering in this life. His compassion and mercy caused him to have a heart for those who were physically hurting, spiritually oppressed, and socially marginalized, and his mercy motivated him to do something about it. As a result, he healed the sick, gave food to the hungry, and comforted those who were exploited. As Matthew observes in his Gospel:

> Jesus traveled through all the towns and villages of that area, teaching in the synagogues and announcing the Good News about the Kingdom. And he healed every kind of disease and illness. When he saw the crowds, he had compassion on them because they were confused and helpless, like sheep without a shepherd (Matthew 9:35-36).

The Edge of His Robe

One healing story in particular has always struck me as being different from the others, but I didn't know why until now. In writing this book, I have discovered that this miracle gets closer to the beauty and wonder of the compassion and healing power of Jesus than any other. It's the story of the woman who had been subject to bleeding for twelve years, likely caused by a menstrual disorder. She was the ultimate outcast because anyone who had contact with her would be considered unclean. Her story is told in all three Synoptic Gospels, but Mark does the best job of explaining her desperate situation and why she came to Jesus.

> She had suffered a great deal from many doctors, and over the years she had spent everything she had to pay them, but she had gotten no better. In fact,

she had gotten worse. She had heard about Jesus, so she came up behind him through the crowd and touched his robe. For she thought to herself, "If I can just touch his robe, I will be healed." Immediately the bleeding stopped, and she could feel in her body that she had been healed of her terrible condition (Mark 5:26-29).

Both Matthew and Luke observe that simply by touching just the fringe or edge of Jesus' robe, the woman was immediately healed (Matthew 9:20; Luke 8:44). This story must have spread throughout the region because Mark later records that people in need of healing followed Jesus wherever he went and tried to touch him as the woman did. "They begged him to let the sick touch at least the fringe of his robe, and all who touched him were healed" (Mark 6:56).

Healing in His Wings

There is a beautiful, poetic Messianic prophecy in Malachi, the last book of the Old Testament, that foreshadows this compassionate healing power of Jesus, the "rising sun" who "will come to us from heaven" (Luke 1:78 NIV):

> "But for you who fear my name, the Sun of Righteousness will rise with healing in his wings. And you will go free, leaping with joy like calves let out to pasture" (Malachi 4:2).

The Hebrew word for "wings" in Malachi has a broader meaning that also includes the "extremity" or "edge" of a wing or a garment. The woman who touched the hem of his garment must have known the prophecy because she had enough faith to recognize Jesus as one who could heal her, and he could do so from the very edge of his robe. Is it any wonder that Jesus told her the reason for her healing?

> "Daughter, your faith has healed you. Go in peace and be freed from your suffering" (Mark 5:34 NIV).

This is Jesus, who stood up in the synagogue in the power of the Spirit and opened the scroll of the prophet Isaiah, proclaiming his authority to heal:

> "The Spirit of the LORD is upon me,
>   for he has anointed me to bring Good News to
>   the poor.
> He has sent me to proclaim that captives will be
> released,
>   that the blind will see,
> that the oppressed will be set free,
>   and that the time of the LORD's favor has come."
>   (Luke 4:18-19)

This is Jesus, who heals the sick, binds up the wounds of the brokenhearted, and sets the captives free.

This is Jesus, who is the ultimate expression of God's love and mercy, whose compassions are new every morning, and whose healing power knows no bounds.

> A vast crowd brought to him people who were lame, blind, crippled, those who couldn't speak, and many others. They laid them before Jesus, and he healed them all. The crowd was amazed! Those who hadn't been able to speak were talking, the crippled were made well, the lame were walking, and the blind

could see again! And they praised the God of Israel (Matthew 15:30-31).

God Heals to Glorify Himself and His Son

The third reason why God heals is to bring glory to himself and to Jesus. When Jesus healed, the people had a natural reaction. As the passage in Matthew demonstrates, they praised the God of Israel. In fact, Jesus had an expectation that the people he healed would glorify God. Remember the ten lepers Jesus healed? As the story goes, he told the ten to show themselves to the priest, and as they went, they were healed. Just one of the ten, who happened to be a Samaritan, came back praising God, threw himself at Jesus' feet, and thanked him. In response, Jesus asked, "Didn't I heal ten men? Where are the other nine? Has no one returned to give glory to God except this foreigner?" (Luke 17:17-18).

HEALING AND FAITH

It is impossible to overlook the role of faith in the healing ministry of Jesus. We already talked about the woman who had been bleeding for twelve years. Jesus told her, "Daughter, your faith has healed you." That same day, two blind men followed Jesus, shouting, "Son of David, have mercy on us!" The two men barged into the house where Jesus was staying, and Jesus asked them, "Do you believe I can make you see?" They told Jesus they believed he could. He then touched their eyes and said, "Because of your faith, it will happen" (Matthew 9:27-29).

On a spiritual level, we know that faith is the key ingredient to salvation. "For it is by grace you have been saved, through faith," the apostle Paul explains. "And this is not from yourselves, it is the gift of God—not by works, so that no one can boast"

(Ephesians 2:8-9 NIV). It's not that God doesn't care about good works, but we can never do enough to make us good enough for God. Only Jesus is good enough, and only Jesus can save us from the death penalty of sin. As Paul writes, "For the wages of sin is death, but the free gift of God is eternal life through Christ Jesus our Lord" (Romans 6:23).

The Bronze Snake

There is a peculiar story in the book of Numbers that best illustrates the role of faith in saving us from death. After rescuing the Israelites from Pharaoh, God brought them into the wilderness, where he gave them his instructions for living. God then led them to the border of the promised land, but they could not enter because they were afraid of "giants in the land." God's people failed to trust God, and as a result they had to stay in the wilderness until the unbelieving generation died out (Numbers 14:26-35).

Fast forward to Numbers 21, when the people begin to complain once again against Moses and God for bringing them into the wilderness. They fail to remember that it was their own sin and unbelief that put them there in the first place. Consequently, God sends "poisonous snakes" among them, and many are bitten and die. The people then come to Moses and ask him to pray that God would take away the snakes. Moses prays, and God instructs him to make a replica of a poisonous snake and attach it to a pole. Moses does as God asks, and the most amazing thing happens. "Anyone who was bitten by a snake could look at the bronze snake and be healed!" (Numbers 21:9).

It might be easy to dismiss this strange episode as one of those Old Testament stories that doesn't have much relevance to us. After all, the story is about those rebellious Israelites. What could that possibly have to do with us? It turns out the story has everything to do with us, and Jesus himself offers an explanation at a time you would least expect.

The most famous verse in the Bible is John 3:16 (NIV): "For God so loved the world that he gave his one and only Son, that whoever believes in him shall not perish but have eternal life." We all know that verse, but how many of us know the two verses that come immediately before? This is Jesus explaining "salvation by faith."

> "As Moses lifted up the bronze snake on a pole in the wilderness, so the Son of Man must be lifted up, so that everyone who believes in him will have eternal life" (John 3:14-15).

Jesus is saying that the bronze snake fashioned by Moses symbolizes him. And just as Moses lifted up the snake on a pole, telling the people to look at it in order to be saved from death caused by their sin, Jesus was lifted up on a pole, with healing in his wings, so that anyone who looks to him by faith will be saved from death caused by sin.

Faith and Our Ultimate Healing

This is the essence of faith. When we believe in Jesus by faith, we will be saved from death, which is the ultimate healing anyone can experience. In the story of the bronze snake in Numbers, faith is described in terms of "looking." Those who were bitten by a poisonous snake had to look at the bronze snake on the pole in order to be saved. The Hebrew word for "looking" in Numbers 21 is not just glancing at or viewing. It means to concentrate on and to be attentive to. In the New Testament, the Greek word for this kind of intent looking is found in Hebrews 12:2, telling us to *look to Jesus* by faith:

> Therefore we also, since we are surrounded by so great a cloud of witnesses, let us lay aside every weight, and the sin which so easily ensnares us, and let us run with endurance the race that is set before us, looking unto Jesus, the author and finisher of our faith, who for the joy that was set before Him endured the cross, despising the shame, and has sat down at the right hand of the throne of God (Hebrews 12:1-2 NKJV).

This act of faith, of looking to Jesus as our only source of spiritual healing, runs counterintuitive to our basic natures. We want to do it ourselves, but God says there's nothing we can do to earn his favor and love. God doesn't want saving faith to depend on us but on Christ alone, the author and finisher of our faith. God doesn't want saving faith to be a product of positive thinking, where our faith requires God to do what we ask. As theologian Wayne Grudem says, "When we come to Christ in faith, we essentially say, 'I give up! I will not depend on myself or my own good works any longer.'"[6]

FAITH HEALING vs. HEALING FAITH

The role of faith in salvation is pretty clear. When it comes to healing, however, the water gets a little muddy. How much faith is required in order for someone to be healed? If we pray and someone is not healed, does that mean we don't have enough faith? Is believing in God for healing different from believing in God for salvation? These are the questions I have wrestled with for many years, and I suspect you have as well, mainly because of the proliferation of so-called faith healers who have become famous by holding meetings, some that attract thousands of people desperate to be healed.

Although it is a global phenomenon, it is not new. Writing more than a hundred years ago, the evangelist and Bible teacher R.A. Torrey had this to say about faith healing:

> There are many who advertise great healings, and many, indeed most, of the healings do not last; and they seek to cast the blame on the one prayed for, saying it is their lack of faith. But that is not Scriptural...The kind of healing that is only temporary and dependent upon the continued faith of the one healed is not Divine healing, not God's healing, but it is Faith Healing, an entirely different matter, a purely psychological process.[7]

The biggest problem with faith healing, according to Torrey, is that it substitutes human faith for God's power. It depends on the faith of the individual rather than the ability of God to heal. It's faith in faith rather than faith in God.

And yet if faith is required for God to heal, what kind of faith does it take for healing to take place? Here are three characteristics or qualities of healing faith.

Faith in God for Healing Means Believing That He Has the Ability to Heal

It's one thing to ask for healing and quite another to actually believe God is able to heal. We referred previously to the story of the two blind men who approach Jesus, boldly asking for healing.

When Jesus asked them, "Do you believe I can make you see?" they answered, "Yes, we do." And Jesus healed them (Matthew 9:28-29).

As I think about my belief in the healing power of God, I can say I believe God is able to heal, but in my heart do I really believe it just like those two blind men? If I do believe God is able to heal, why do I pray that God will use doctors and medicine to heal someone going through an illness rather than believing that God can instantly heal the one I am praying for?

A friend of mine was facing surgery to remove a cancerous tumor. I prayed that the doctors would find and remove the cancer and that it would not spread. But if I really believed God has the ability to heal, why didn't I pray that the tumor would disappear without medical intervention?

I am not discounting the role of the medical profession in bringing people back to health. In fact, the history of medicine could not be written without the influence of Christians motivated by the love and compassion of Jesus for the sick. The first hospitals were established in the fourth century by the Christian church. Florence Nightingale, the founder of modern nursing, was a devout Christian woman. Missionary organizations have constructed thousands of hospitals all over the world, and Christian medical teams are often the first to respond to a critical health crisis.

But if I put all of my belief in God's healing in the context of modern medicine, haven't I become a kind of "healing deist" who believes God has removed himself from our world, leaving it to doctors and relief agencies to alleviate the sickness and suffering in our world? I may still believe that God *can* heal, but am I hedging my bet when I pray for healing because I don't really have the faith to believe that God *will* heal?

Faith in God for Healing Means Believing It Is His Will to Heal

Praying with faith that God will heal is different from asking if it is God's will to heal. Often when we pray for something, whether it's healing or something else, we often qualify our prayer by adding, "If it is your will." A friend once told me that she doesn't like to pray with that qualifier because it shows a lack of faith. I don't agree. Even Jesus prayed that way when he said before going to the cross, "Father, if you are willing, please take this cup of suffering away from me. Yet I want your will to be done, not mine" (Luke 22:42-43).

Just because we believe God *can* do something doesn't mean he *must*. God is not obligated to heal just because we ask. That would be faith that depends on us rather than faith that depends on God. Even Jesus recognized this. Praying by faith means praying in the will of God, which is basically asking God if he is willing.

You see this pattern in the way Jesus responds to those who asked him for healing. Once a man with leprosy approached Jesus and knelt before him, saying "Lord, if you are willing, you can heal me and make me clean." Jesus then reached out and touched him, saying, "I am willing." The man was instantly healed (Matthew 8:1-3). Praying for healing in the will of God means that we understand that healing depends on God, not us.

Faith in God for Healing Means Believing Anything Is Possible

My wife suffers from moderately severe scoliosis. Rather than being straight like most of us, her spine is deformed into the shape of an *S*. I worry about her back and pray for her constantly, but I have never prayed for her spine to be made straight. Why not? Do I doubt that God could heal her in that way? In my head, I don't doubt God's ability to heal, but in my heart I don't believe he *will* straighten her spine. It just seems too extreme. And if I'm being honest, it's more than that. I believe God can give my wife relief from her pain, but I don't believe he can straighten her spine because it seems *impossible.* Consequently, I've never prayed that way.

I should be ashamed, not just before my wife, but before God.

Since when is anything impossible for God? He created the universe for crying out loud. The prophet Jeremiah observes this very fact when it comes to God's ability to do anything:

> "O Sovereign LORD! You made the heavens and earth
> by your strong hand and powerful arm. Nothing is
> too hard for you!" (Jeremiah 32:17).

A few verses later, God confirms this fact:

> "I am the LORD, the God of all the peoples of the world.
> Is anything too hard for me?" (Jeremiah 32:27).

Jesus confirms this as well when the father of a boy possessed by an evil spirit pleads with Jesus, "Have mercy on us and help us, if you can." Jesus is incredulous. "What do you mean, 'If I can'?" he asks the boy's father. "Anything is possible if a person believes." To that the father instantly cries out, "I do believe, but help me overcome my unbelief!" (Mark 9:22-24).

That father is me. When I pray for others, too often I am a mixture of faith and unbelief. Yet as I read how Jesus responded to the fragile faith of this desperate father, I know he will respond to me with the same compassion and power. And I know he will respond to you.

It's not faith in our ability; it's faith in God's ability. It's not our will but his. And it's not our faith that hinders us, but our failure to believe that with God, all things are possible.

There is no person Jesus won't heal. There is no place Jesus will not go. And there is no power Jesus will not overcome.

I do believe, Lord, but help me overcome my unbelief!

CHAPTER 5

When God Does (or Doesn't) Heal

While my father lay dying in a hospital bed in his hometown of Mountain Lake, Minnesota, his older sister Ruth was in the process of being miraculously healed nearly six thousand miles away in the African country of Ivory Coast. Ruth had life-threatening digestive issues, and the closest doctor was four hours away. Knowing she needed immediate help, the Africans came together and prayed for her healing. "We're going to ask for a miracle," they said as they stretched out on the floor around her. In the middle of the prayer, Ruth saw a light. "I saw it as an abundance of power," she told me. "I knew then that God was going to heal me."

After the prayer, Ruth got into a truck to make the four-hour journey to see the doctor, and she forgot the belt she had been wearing to alleviate the pain. Ruth was in the process of retrieving the belt when she heard God's voice. "That's when God told me, 'Aren't you going to believe me?' So, I threw the belt into the fire. At that point I began feeling fingers around my stomach."

Ruth saw the doctor and told him she was being healed. A scan showed her abdomen was distended and displaced. "The doctor mocked me and told me to return the next day," Ruth said.

She returned as requested and the doctor scanned her once again. "Unbelievable," he told her. "Your stomach is moving." Indeed, Ruth was in the process of being completely healed.

Days later Ruth sent a letter to her family back home describing her healing. My father read the letter while he was in the hospital. His sister had been healed. Within weeks he would die.

One of the most perplexing aspects of the healing power of God is that it doesn't always happen, at least not the way we think it should. Maybe this is why I haven't yet prayed for my wife's spine to become straight but choose instead to pray for her comfort. I don't want to be in the position of saying that God hasn't healed her.

By comparison, Lee Strobel's wife suffers from a neurobiological disorder that gives her constant pain. "Have we prayed for relief from her pain?" Strobel writes. "Continually. Have we beseeched God for his healing? *Often and frequently.* Have we seen any improvement? *Quite the opposite.*"[1]

The result of years of crying out for healing with no apparent answer has caused Strobel to express frustration "that God performs healings in some circumstances but not others."[2] I know the feeling. God healed my aunt Ruth, who is still living at ninety-two years old, but he didn't heal my father, who died at the age of twenty-six.

Even though the circumstances of my own family happened when I was a child, the effect still lingers. Why did God heal my aunt but not my father, especially when he believed with all his heart that he would be healed, whereas my aunt's healing was initiated by others? Is it possible that circumstances dictated the outcome, or was there something more personal involved? Before we look at some possible answers, let's consider some outright hindrances to healing.

HINDRANCES TO HEALING

When it comes to healing, we have a tendency to get in our own way. We pray for healing, believing that God will answer, and then end up frustrated and disappointed when he doesn't. In these situations, we look to God for reasons why he doesn't heal, when in reality we should be looking at ourselves. As I've thought about it, here are three hindrances to healing that come from us, not from God.

We Are Worried About How We Will Look

I have already admitted this hindrance in my own life. I'm concerned that if I pray for my wife's spine to be straightened, I will be embarrassed, even if my wife is the only one who notices. In effect, my ego is the hindrance to her healing. "Worrying how we look when we pray for the sick is not a very effective way of getting our prayers answered," writes Jack Deere. "That is because God is not primarily concerned about how we look."[3] God won't heal anyone to keep us from looking foolish. "He will, however, heal someone to bring glory to his Son."[4]

We Have Been Jaded by Celebrity Faith Healers

I touched on this in the last chapter, but it bears repeating here because celebrity faith healers are a hindrance rather than a help to the healing power of God. The sad reality is that faith healers and other proponents of the prosperity gospel take advantage of people who are desperate for God's healing power by guaranteeing that God will answer their prayers if they have enough faith. In a widely circulated article in the *New York Times*, "Death, the Prosperity Gospel and Me," Kate Bowler had this to say about these manipulative tactics:

> The prosperity gospel popularized a Christian expla-
> nation for why some people make it and some do
> not. They revolutionized prayer as an instrument
> for getting God to always say "yes." It offers people
> a guarantee: Follow these rules, and God will reward
> you, heal you, restore you.[5]

Bowler writes from personal experience. Her book *Blessed* is a thoroughly researched study of the prosperity gospel movement. She wrote a follow-up book, *Everything Happens for a Reason*, after being diagnosed with stage IV colon cancer. In an interview following the book's publication, Bowler articulated the shallow perspective of this movement. "I spent so long studying the pros- perity gospel—the idea that God wants to bless you with health and wealth and happiness," she answered, "that I think I had really gotten used to it as this sort of synthetic explanation for the good and the bad stuff that comes up in your life."[6]

There's no question that many have the gift of healing, but the moment someone engaged in a healing ministry goes from relative anonymity to outright celebrity, the ministry ceases to be effective (if it was ever effective in the first place). "One of the clues that some present-day healing ministries are in significant trouble is the celebrity status given to and accepted by those who have been used in significant healings," Deere observes. He further states,

> I believe that some people who advertise great heal-
> ing ministries are frauds. I believe that others, at the

> beginning of their ministry, were used in a signifi-
> cant way by the Lord for healing and miracles. But
> along the way they allowed themselves to become
> deceived, and now they are promoting themselves
> more than the Son of God. That kind of promo-
> tion may get large crowds and bring in significant
> amounts of money, but it does not please the Lord.[7]

Do you wonder why Jesus often told the person he just healed, "Don't tell anyone" (see Luke 8:56 as an example)? You would think the publicity generated by giving sight to the blind and making the crippled walk again would have been good for the earthly ministry of Jesus. But that's not the way he saw it. Torrey writes,

> The Lord Jesus Himself never held Divine Healing
> meetings. He did heal many. He did heal people
> in crowds (because He was fulfilling prophecy as
> to the signs that would accompany the Messiah),
> but He never advertised such meetings, but rather
> avoided as far as He could all such public manifes-
> tations of His healing powers. He strictly charged
> those whom He healed to keep still about it, lest
> men should make Him a mere Healer, and not what
> He really was, a Teacher and the Savior of the world.[8]

The last thing Jesus wanted to become was a celebrity. He was all about glorifying his Father, not drawing attention to himself.

We Don't Really Want to Get Well

You may question this third hindrance, but have you ever been sick, maybe not so sick that you needed divine healing, but sick enough that your condition elicited sympathy from those around you? When this happens, sometimes your illness becomes your identity, if only for a period of time. While you are sick, people pay attention to you and shower you with kindness, well wishes, and prayers. When you get better, they move on, leaving you to go back to your healthy and ordinary life. As strange as it seems, you kind of miss your sickness.

Once Jesus encountered a man who had been paralyzed for thirty-eight years. Without question his affliction was his identity. Every day he would show up at a pool in Jerusalem called Bethesda. "Here a great number of disabled people used to lie—the blind, the lame, the paralyzed" (John 5:3 NIV). Among this throng of people, Jesus focused on one paralyzed man. "Do you want to get well," he asked him. The man told Jesus that he had no one to put him in the water while it was "stirred," which likely means that people believed the water had some kind of healing power.

Only Jesus has the power to heal, but he needed to know if this paralyzed man wanted to get well. Did he want to cling to his broken identity or did he want to be healed? Seeing that the man did want healing, Jesus told him, "Get up! Pick up your mat and walk" (John 5:8 NIV).

My wife and I have been to Jerusalem, and we visited the pool of Bethesda, in the middle of an area where five massive colonnades used to stand. There's a plaque by the pool with the verse from John 5:8, followed by this statement in both French and English:

> *Jesus is all-powerful, omnipotent.*
> *He always has ways*
> *and means to help you.*

WAYS AND MEANS TO HELP US

My father died of cancer, specifically Hodgkin's disease

(known today as Hodgkin's lymphoma) in the mid-1950s. When he was diagnosed, there were no successful treatments available for this type of cancer, at least not like we have today. In my grandfather's personal diary, he wrote that my father—his son—was given "mustard treatments." It sounds primitive, but there was a form of cancer treatment in those days that used a nitrogen mustard compound.

I will never know if nitrogen mustard would have eradicated the cancer because my father initially refused treatment. He believed that receiving the best medical science had to offer would have demonstrated a lack of faith. Only recently have I discovered from my aunt Ruth that my mother was distressed with my father's decision. She pleaded with him to change his mind. Eventually he relented, and the two of them traveled from Minnesota to Texas to get the nitrogen mustard treatment.

Ironically, my father was in the hospital in Mountain Lake recovering from the procedure when he received and read the letter my aunt Ruth sent from Africa announcing her healing.

I don't blame my father for choosing to trust God rather than medicine for his healing. I don't know the circumstances surrounding his illness, and it's impossible to read his heart. The best clues come from his collection of books, many written about the Holy Spirit by writers I have come to admire: A.B. Simpson, D.L. Moody, Andrew Murray, and R.A. Torrey. In fact, the discovery of these books prompted me to write *Fire and Wind: Unleashing the Power and Presence of the Holy Spirit.*[9]

Of these writers, R.A. Torrey stands out for his teaching on the healing power of God. Torrey was a renowned evangelist who toured the world preaching the gospel in the late nineteenth and early twentieth centuries. He became the pastor of the famed

Moody Church in Chicago before accepting the position of dean at the Bible Institute of Los Angeles, now Biola University, in 1912. It's possible that Torrey's teaching on whether or not God uses "means" to heal influenced my father in one way or another. Here's what Torrey has to say about the role of medicine in our healing:

> Now there arises a question of great practical importance. Is the use of all medical or other therapeutic means wrong for one who believes in Divine Healing? Sometimes it is, sometimes it is not. Sometimes if you go to God in prayer for the healing of self or others and then use means, when the healing comes the medicine or the doctor gets all the glory and God none.[10]

Maybe my father wanted God to get all the glory for his healing. His speech in front of the Wheaton student body seems to confirm that idea. At the same time, did my father overlook a practical dimension of healing that is less spectacular but just as effective? Torrey acknowledges the use of medicine as perfectly acceptable as a means to heal. "Our Lord Jesus occasionally used means in connection with His cures," he writes. "He used clay and spittle for eyes that could not see."[11] Torrey also refers to the apostle Paul recommending to Timothy, "You ought to drink a little wine for the sake of your stomach because you are sick so often" (1 Timothy 5:23).

Torrey was not a fan of medicine, but he also understood the value of medical science to bring about healing:

> It certainly does not honor God to refuse all remedies and get steadily worse and at the same time

to say you are trusting God for healing. And many die doing it and bring great reproach upon God and upon Christianity and upon the great truth of Divine Healing.[12]

THE HEALING POWER OF GOD

We will talk about "the great truth of Divine Healing" in the next chapter, but first I want to share three stories of healing that have come into my experience over the last few years. Each one is different, but all vividly demonstrate the healing power of God. My hope is that as you read these stories, you will gain a sense of the goodness, the grace, the love, and the imagination of our great God.

Healing as a Process

Dr. Dave Horner is a professor of philosophy and biblical studies at Talbot School of Theology at Biola University, a leading Christian university founded in 1908. Basically, Dave studies and teaches the Bible for a living, yet there was a time when holding a Bible endangered his life. No, it wasn't because Dave once lived in a country where it is illegal to own a Bible. It was the Bible itself—the pages and ink and the chemicals in both—that caused his body to quite literally shut down. And Dave's negative physical reaction wasn't restricted to Bibles. Handling any book, especially old ones, could severely weaken him.

Dave has an immune system disorder, which basically means his immune system doesn't work the way it should. Dave believes his condition was caused by mold toxicity that invaded his body at a time when he worked in a foundry full of chemicals as he was putting himself through school. In addition, Dave contracted

Lyme disease, severely compromising his immune system. In fact, tests have shown that he has no immune system.

When Dave first began seeking medical help, the doctors thought he had a tumor (he didn't). After he began teaching, an ear, nose, and throat doctor performed surgery to remove polyps, which helped a little. But as soon as he returned to his office at Biola, full of books and Bibles, the symptoms returned. Dave seriously thought about wearing a hazmat suit but decided the sight of a professor dressed as though he were in the middle of a chemical waste dump might distract his students.

His department arranged for him to move from his old office to a newly constructed building on the Biola campus, where supposedly no mold was present. To be on the safe side, Dave wrapped his books in plastic bags, and he started reading from an electronic version of the Bible. At home, Dave did everything possible to insulate himself from various mold sources. He installed a special air-conditioning filter and sealed the foundation. Then, in the midst of his own trauma, Dave's wife, Debbie, was diagnosed with cancer. "I lost hope," he told me.

Debbie's treatment was effective, but Dave's condition worsened. He had to drop out of speaking engagements, including one on the topic of hope. "I couldn't do it," he said. "My blood pressure was spiking, and I couldn't sleep. I was being beaten to death every day."

Late in 2018, Dave told his department chair that he could not continue to teach, that he would need to go on disability. "By this point, my physical condition was so bad it even impaired my reading, but I was desperate, so I started reading books about my condition." One book in particular, *You Are Not Your Brain* by Jeffrey Schwartz, a research psychiatrist at the UCLA School of Medicine, explained how the brain is involved in our health through the limbic system. "The brain can literally program our bodies to produce a certain response," Dave explained. "For me, just the thought of perfume had an adverse effect on both my physical and emotional state."

Dave and Debbie also searched for specialists who could help him. They learned about a doctor in Florida who specializes in toxicity and Lyme disease, but the cost was $100,000. That was not an option. At this point, the only option Dave considered was accepting an early retirement offer from Biola University, which meant he could retire and receive a full year's salary.

The deadline for accepting the offer was swiftly approaching when Dave and Debbie met a couple who told them about a church in Georgia called Hope of the Generations, pastored by Henry Wright. Dave told me he had never heard of Henry Wright, the church, or Henry Wright's book *A More Excellent Way*, which teaches that human problems (including physical ailments) are fundamentally spiritual, with physical and psychological manifestations.[13]

The deadline for taking early retirement was May 3, but Debbie told Dave to "say no by faith" to the offer. The next day, Dave and Debbie were on their way to Hope of the Generations Church in Georgia, where they would spend a week with seventy other people who had various emotional, spiritual, and physical needs, including cancer. Different pastors spoke and spent time with the attendees, encouraging them to record their experiences. Henry Wright alone knew Dave's condition, but others in the church knew how to pray and what to tell Dave.

"I learned about demon deliverance," Dave said. "Dark spiritual forces are out to eat your lunch, and I discovered that there's a chance I had a spirit of fear talking to me. Perfectionism, unforgiveness, self-rejection—these are the manifestations of a broken heart, and they were the evidence that I had been cooperating with a spirit of fear."

On the last day, Henry Wright spoke to the group, telling them Jesus came to defeat the works of the devil (1 John 3:8). Wright had written a sheet for each person, so the individual prayers were very specific. "It was all pretty informal," Dave remarked. "They asked permission to lay hands on me." Throughout the week, Dave noticed some changes. "My voice got stronger, and I felt a progressive lightening. It wasn't instantaneous, but I felt a release."

When Dave and Debbie returned home, Dave went to his favorite coffee shop and felt the same thing coming back. Immediately he "rebuked" the spirit of fear that had been holding him in bondage. Dave quoted Luke 13:12, where Jesus heals a crippled woman, saying to her, "Woman, you are set free from your infirmity" (NIV). Then Jesus put his hands on her, "and immediately she straightened up and praised God" (Luke 13:13 NIV).

Dave also referenced *The Bondage Breaker* by Neil Anderson, a classic book that offers a holistic and biblical approach to spiritual warfare.[14] "Setting people free from spiritual captivity and bondage is why Jesus came," Dave told me, referencing Isaiah 61:1, a prophecy concerning the coming Messiah:

> The Spirit of the Sovereign LORD is upon me,
>   for the LORD has anointed me
>   to bring good news to the poor.
> He has sent me to comfort the brokenhearted
>   and to proclaim that captives will be released
>   and prisoners will be freed.

Seven hundred years later Jesus would go to the synagogue and read this same passage from the scroll of Isaiah, concluding with this statement affirming his identity as the true Bondage Breaker: "The Scripture you've just heard has been fulfilled this very day!" (Luke 4:21).

As for Dave, his bondage to toxicity has indeed been broken. No longer is he being held captive by his debilitating physical ailment. No longer does he live with a spirit of fear. Dave has been healed. He has been set free.

Healing in an Instant

Because I travel so much, I am dependent on ride-sharing services for my transportation to and from airports around the world. Over the last few years I have experienced hundreds of rides from hundreds of drivers, but none like Daniel.

I enjoy learning about the various backgrounds of the drivers who pick me up, and often they will ask what I do. That's what Daniel did, and when I told him I was involved with Christian publishing, he launched into an amazing healing story.

"I used to drive a limo," Daniel said, "and one night I was assaulted while driving four girls from a homecoming dance." He was driving in a residential neighborhood when three "young punks" threw a bottle at the limo, barely missing the partially opened window in back where the girls were sitting. Daniel stopped the limo and got out to confront the gang. Bad idea.

The three punks went into full-attack mode, kicking and punching Daniel. One guy hit him with such force that Daniel flipped over a chest-high fence. That's when another punk pulled out a knife and stabbed Daniel in the heart. "I got stabbed in the left ventricle," he said. "The doctors told me later that a wound to the left ventricle is almost always fatal."

At this point I'm looking at my driver in disbelief, my mouth fully open. Obviously, Daniel survived the stabbing, but how?

"I'm lying there thinking about my life and my wife and how I can't say goodbye to her," Daniel continued. "And it occurs to me that I need to get right by God. I knew about God and believed in him, but I couldn't remember the last time I prayed. I'm starting to fade because I'm bleeding internally, but I had enough awareness to pray and ask God for help. I ended my prayer by saying, 'In Jesus' name.' Suddenly a calm came over me and my head got clear. I could feel something at the top of my head, and then strength came to my body. I was able to get up and look for someone to help me."

"And here you are," I told him.

"Yes, here I am," he responded, a big smile on his face.

I asked him how he was doing with God now.

"Well, I'm following the Lord, as are all six of my stepchildren and my stepfather," he said. "I don't preach to them, just try to set an example." I asked Daniel if he's told his story to many people. He has, but he'd like to tell more. He has some inventions he would like to develop, then use the money to buy an RV so he can travel the country and tell his story of healing to whoever will listen.

I hope and pray Daniel is able to do that, and I told him so as he dropped me off.

Eternal Healing

There were seven of us in a Bible study. Three were pastors from different church traditions—Baptist, Presbyterian, and Greek Orthodox. Two were in law enforcement. I was managing the Christian bookstore chain my family owned, and the seventh member, Curt, was an executive with a communications company.

Curt was the one we all looked up to, and not just because he was taller and better looking than the rest of us. He was a successful corporate leader with outsized portions of integrity, charisma, and generosity the rest of us could only aspire to.

When Curt was diagnosed with brain cancer, all of us were heartbroken. All except Curt, who stood tall and resolute. He told us God was in control. On the eve of the day the doctors would operate, our group of seven held a healing service in Curt's home. I had never been part of something like this on such an intimate level, and from the outset I was tentative—not doubtful, just unsure. I am somewhat embarrassed to admit that to you now, but I need to continue being transparent with you.

If I was confident that night, it was in the fact that three ministers from three different churches were there. Father Jim, the dear Greek Orthodox priest, was designated to lead our private healing service. And why not? If you know anything about the Orthodox tradition, you know they have a liturgy—including incense, candles, and ancient texts—to fit the occasion of every need. I was impressed and deeply moved.

But I was still tentative, and here's why. Out of the seven of us, I didn't want to be the weak link. Even as Father Jim anointed Curt with oil on the very spot where the surgeon's knife would cut in the morning, I trembled internally. *Lord, don't let my weak faith be a hindrance to Curt's healing,* I prayed.

After the surgery, we all continued to pray for Curt, and then came the news we all dreaded. The surgery did not get all of the tumor, and the cancer was still spreading. The prognosis was not good. Curt was discharged and sent home, where his health steadily declined. We continued to pray but feared the worst.

A few weeks after his surgery, Karin and I went to see Curt, and I will never forget the feeling of walking into his home, his wife, Mary, ever strong beside him. Curt was sitting in his favorite chair, looking gaunt because of weight loss, his head downcast. Mary told us he had lost some of his sight, but when he heard our voices, he lifted his head and smiled.

We greeted Curt, and then I blurted out a question I had not planned to ask at that moment, but I couldn't help myself. In hindsight, it was probably a selfish inquiry meant to assuage my own guilt for possibly being the one person out of the seven who didn't have enough faith to prompt God to heal my friend.

"Curt," I asked quietly, "are you disappointed that God didn't heal you?" My voice was shaking as I uttered those words. Instantly Curt straightened in his chair as best he could and looked at me intently.

"What are you talking about?" he asked. Stunned by his response, I had no reply. Clearly Curt had not been healed. What was I missing?

Then the Lord, the same Lord who declared to the Israelites, "I am the one who heals you," spoke through Curt, and the words were aimed directly at me. "God has healed me in ways you can't even imagine," he declared. "I don't want you to worry about me. God is in control. All will be well."

Without missing a beat, Curt continued with a simple yet profound explanation. "This is how God has healed me. He is using my life to touch others with his love. As long as I live, I want God to use me."

His words were prophetic. Over the next few weeks of Curt's

life, God used him to shine his love on dozens of people who visited him, even as the cancer continued to ravage his body. His memorial service, directed by Father Jim, was both mournful and filled with hope. The church was packed with several hundred people, many of them Curt's professional colleagues, some no doubt hearing the gospel for the very first time.

Curt had indeed been healed, but not for this world. Curt experienced the healing we will all experience someday, the complete healing of body, soul, and spirit that will most assuredly come when we see our Savior face-to-face.

CHAPTER 6

How to Experience the Healing Power of God

The father of a good friend was in constant pain. He had been to doctors and tried their remedies, but nothing worked. One evening he was listening to a preacher on the radio. He wasn't a prosperity preacher as such, but he talked about God's healing power. On this particular night the preacher said that anyone suffering physically should put their hands on the radio so they would feel the healing touch of God.

My friend's father had never done anything like this before, but he was hurting. So he did the thing the preacher asked and put his hand on the little radio in his kitchen as the preacher prayed, his voice coming through the scratchy speaker in the night. Suddenly, as my friend's father closed his eyes and offered his own prayer, something strange happened. Something he could feel right there in his body, in the kitchen. The feeling started in his fingertips and then coursed throughout his body, and when the preacher was done praying, the pain was gone, never to return.

Several times in this book I have cautioned against the excesses and at times the deception of the prosperity gospel and faith healers. Truthfully, those warnings could apply to any branch of Christianity. In our attempts to create programs and institutions that ostensibly help people get closer to God, we sometimes stumble. Human ambition and ego can get in the way. False doctrine can creep in. Luke, the writer of the book of Acts, commended the people of Berea, who "searched the Scriptures day after day to see if Paul and Silas were teaching the truth" (Acts 17:11). The implication is that we are responsible to discern truth from error.

At the same time, it's possible to take things to the extreme and discount the way some practice their faith simply because we are uncomfortable with their style. In this case, our discerning spirit becomes a critical one, and we miss seeing God at work in ways that may be highly effective, if unconventional.

And what is "conventional" anyway? Too often, it's information or experiences that line up with what we're comfortable with. Anything outside the normal boundaries of the beliefs and traditions we have learned and practiced is suspect, so we discount if not condemn the person and their ministry.

I'm afraid that's what I've done with some who claim to have a special conduit to the healing power of God. I want to experience God's healing touch for myself and for others, but I want the process of accessing that healing to fit into my theological worldview. And where has it gotten me? For the most part, my life has been largely devoid of the supernatural manifestations of God. Consequently, if I truly want to feel the healing touch of God—not just once but always—maybe I need to be more open to God's unconventional ways.

Kate Bowler understands this, which is why she gives credit to the practice of some prosperity preachers who offer God's healing touch to people. "The prosperity gospel understands the power of touch perhaps better than anyone," she writes. "The earliest prosperity preachers were tent revivalists who used to get down into the crowd at the pinnacle of the service, rolling up their sleeves to lay their hands on the heads and limbs of trembling believers."[1]

Bowler mentions the famed televangelist Oral Roberts, who "used to raise his right hand to the camera so viewers could press their hands against the screen. The next best thing to skin on skin."[2] The father of my friend who was healed after putting his hand on the radio is evidence of this virtual healing touch of God.

GOD IS NOT PREDICTABLE

In the last chapter I told three stories of healing: Dave's story of being healed over time, Daniel's story of instant healing, and Curt's story of God having something better in mind. Of the three stories, I probably struggled most to understand Dave's story and why it unfolded the way it did.

When I heard about Dave's healing, I set up an appointment to meet with him so I could hear his story firsthand. Not knowing anything about the long ordeal he had been through, I went to our meeting expecting to hear that someone had prayed for him, and *voila!* he was healed. But that was not Dave's experience. Instead, his healing was drawn out over a period of time, somewhat chaotic and wholly unpredictable.

I will admit that initially I was mildly disappointed that Dave didn't describe his healing as following some preconceived notion I had in mind, such as a group of church elders getting together to pray for him (as we read about in James 5:14-15). It was much more complicated than that, which is precisely what drew me in.

As Dave's story unfolded, I found myself in utter wonder over the extravagance and unpredictability of his healing. It was not "conventional," if by conventional we mean the kinds of miracles that fit the "characteristics of a true miracle" (see chapter 2).

And that's when it hit me.

It seems to me that Christians of all stripes are guilty of trying to reduce God to formulas and conventions, especially when it comes to his healing power. If we're Presbyterian (like me), we pray that God will use doctors to heal those who are sick. If we're charismatic, we pray that God will use someone to place their hands on the one who is sick so he or she can instantly be healed. And if we're Baptist, we just avoid the topic altogether (just kidding...sort of).

Vanishing Transcendence

My point is that we are more comfortable putting God in a neat and tidy category rather than accepting him for who he is. We want God to be practical and predictable. That way, when we need him for a particular task, we simply ask for his help and expect him to respond the way we think he should, rather than accepting and seeking him for who he really is. Sadly, we have bought into the philosophy of popular books and speakers from the general culture who encourage us to take control of our lives and make things happen rather than allowing outside forces to dictate what we should believe and how we need to behave. We have reduced God to a formula and our faith to a system.

In his book *Into the Depths of God*, the preacher/poet Calvin Miller laments the "loss of transcendence" in the way we relate to God. "Secular culture is stripping the church of the last otherworldly shreds of a vanishing transcendence," he writes.[3] God delights in going beyond ordinary limits, of surpassing our expectations, and yet we prefer to keep him tamed and available for those times when we need him. "We have become the plain, pragmatic people," Miller continues, and this is no way to relate to God. "We must quit making God a practical deity who exists to help us succeed."[4]

Glorious Chaos

This stripping away of God's transcendence inevitably influences the way we approach healing. Miller was asked to speak at a Pentecostal church, and the pastor encouraged him to give an invitation at the conclusion of his sermon, which he did. "I've been a Baptist for a long time," recounts Miller. "I was used to seeing nobody come forward even after multiple verses of 'Just As I Am.' It scared me to see so many of them coming."[5]

And come they did. They came forward in droves, some with a desire to give their lives to Christ and others who were sick and wanted prayer for healing. The pastor said to Miller, "I will counsel the lost, would you take care of the healing?" Miller's response to this request is worth quoting in its entirety:

> "Please, Pastor," I begged. "I'm a Baptist. I don't do healing. When we Baptists get sick, we take pills. I'm not good at healing."
>
> "Just pray for the sick—that's all you have to do, just pray."
>
> So I did. In thirty or forty minutes the chaos was over, but I will never forget that overwhelming feeling that there were people all over the place and God was doing things in their lives. I have many times blessed this glorious chaos. And now I know what was missing in Ephesus. I know where Apollos fell short. I know the glory of divine mayhem that

comes in the visitation of God, and it is not always orderly.[6]

I love Miller's description of the "glorious chaos" and "divine mayhem" of God and the way he works in the world and in our lives. Rather than trying to get a handle on God so we can get a direct and immediate benefit, we need to embrace and worship and pray to the magnificent, unbound, unpredictable, and sometimes chaotic God who loves us unconditionally and longs to touch us with his extravagant love.

Dave's story of healing confirmed all of these characteristics. God offers healing and hope to each of his children, but not in the ways we might expect. As I continue to think about Dave, I have found my imagination opening up. I have begun to think more about God in supernatural terms, touching the world, touching me.

HOW DOES GOD TOUCH US?

We may think that we are the ones who long for the healing touch of God. Did you ever consider that God wants us to touch him as well? He longs to have a relationship with us so that we can feel his love and experience his intimate care. We talked in chapter 3 about the miracle of the incarnation, when immaterial God became material flesh. Jesus was and remains God in human form, standing at the right hand of the Father, praying and pleading to God on our behalf (Romans 8:34).

As we observed previously, when Jesus was on earth, his touch was an intricate and an intimate part of his healing ministry. After he gave his Sermon on the Mount, Jesus healed a man with leprosy, considered "untouchable" because of his disease. Yet Jesus "reached out and touched him" (Matthew 8:3). When

Jesus visited Peter's sick mother-in-law, he "took her by the hand, and helped her sit up" (Mark 1:31). Once Jesus encountered a boy possessed by an evil spirit that had robbed him of speech. Jesus rebuked the impure spirit and then, after the spirit had left the boy, he "took him by the hand and helped him to his feet" (Mark 9:27).

Jesus is no longer with us in the physical sense, but he has not left us alone. His presence and touch are still with us in the form of the Holy Spirit, the third person of the Trinity. In *Fire and Wind*, my book about experiencing the power and presence of the Holy Spirit, I write,

> When you are with a person, you are in the *presence* of that person. That's the way the disciples felt when they were with Jesus. They were in his presence. They heard his voice and observed his actions firsthand, including the miracles he performed. But Jesus could only be with them when he was *with* them. After Jesus ascended into heaven, the Holy Spirit became then, and continues to be, the presence of Jesus in us. Even more, the Holy Spirit is the presence of the Trinity—Father, Son, and Holy Spirit—in us and among us.[7]

When Nicodemus came to Jesus in the night, wanting to know more about the one who was doing miracles, Jesus told him he needed to be "born again." According to Jesus, the way this happens is through the Holy Spirit, who touches us like the wind touches everything in its path (John 3:7-8). The words in Hebrew (*ruach*) and Greek (*pneuma*) are the same for wind, breath, and spirit:

- the "Spirit of God hovering over the waters" at the dawn of creation (Genesis 1:2)

- the Lord God breathing "the breath of life into the man's nostrils," and the man becoming "a living person" (Genesis 2:7)

- the wind that blows "wherever it wants," the wind that shows we are "born of the Spirit" (John 3:8)

This is also the same breath—the breath of God—that inspired the prophets to write the Scriptures (2 Timothy 3:16; 2 Peter 1:20-21). This is the same Spirit who helps us understand those Scriptures (John 16:13). And this is the same Holy Spirit who "helps us in our weakness" and prays on our behalf with deep emotion when we don't know "what God wants us to pray for" (Romans 8:26-27).

This is God the Father, Son, and Holy Spirit touching our lives. How this happens and how we feel it is sometimes mysterious, unpredictable and, yes, gloriously chaotic. But this touch of God in every dimension of his being is just what we need. For too long we have relied on our own systems and predictable outcomes. It's time we embraced the glory of God in all his splendor, right here, right now where we live and move and have our being. Writing in the *Image Journal*, the philosopher and Augustinian scholar James K.A. Smith beautifully expresses this way of living:

> Commenting on Saint Paul's assertion in Romans 8 that the Spirit sighs with groans too deep for words, Augustine remarks: "There is therefore in us a certain learned ignorance, so to speak—an ignorance which we learn from that Spirit of God who helps our infirmities." For many of us—perhaps especially

in our cultural moment, after modernity—this learned ignorance is most germane. It's an unknowing for those who so confidently "know," who seem to have mastered the world. We need to be unsettled, disrupted, decentered. Unknowing can have its own epiphany.[8]

An intimate relationship directly with God is not only possible but preferable. I confess I have lived my Christian life with God as a boss, the teacher in a classroom, and life advisor. Consequently, my priorities have been focused on how to please him by my performance. So I read the Bible dutifully and pray with a list in my hand, asking God for things, including the healing of others and, when I need it, myself. But when I treat God this way—as a teacher, advisor, and provider—I am not relating to him as a living *person* who acts in real time and wants to touch me even as he wants to be touched by me.

Dallas Willard offers a sharp perspective (and rebuke) to my errant way of relating to God.

> We demean God immeasurably by casting him in the role of cosmic boss, foreman or autocrat, whose chief joy in relation to humans is to order them around, taking pleasure in seeing them jump at his command and painstakingly noting any failures. Instead, we are to be God's friends (2 Chronicles 20:7; John 15:13-15) and fellow workers (1 Corinthians 3:9, NASB).[9]

BECOMING FRIENDS WITH GOD

The touch of God begins with our friendship with God.

Unquestionably we have undervalued this way of knowing and experiencing God. And yet if we just look to the Scriptures and identify those characters who are most admirable and worthy of imitation, we inevitably discover they had a friendship with God.

Let's take Moses as a prime example. Aside from Jesus, no one in the Bible had a more direct and dynamic relationship with God than Moses. God first appeared to Moses in a burning bush (Exodus 3). In the years following that seminal moment, God and Moses talked like two old friends. Yes, there were assignments and commands and corrections, but there was also an intimacy and familiarity that we should envy. Whether it was in Egypt or on Mount Sinai or in the wilderness, God and Moses had a real friendship going on. Wouldn't you love to have this written of you?

> The LORD would speak to Moses face to face, as one
> speaks to a friend (Exodus 33:11).

Do you know it's possible? You can speak to God as one speaks to a friend. We need to first accept that God desires to speak to us and interact with us, and then, as Dallas Willard advises, we need to read and study the Bible with "the assumption that the experiences recorded there are basically the same type as ours would have been if we had been there."[10]

I am in the process of reading through the Bible by following a wonderful Bible reading experience called Immerse, which invites all who participate "to discover God's story and then to step into it."[11] I started with the complete New Testament (called *Immerse: Messiah*) and then moved to the Old Testament with *Immerse: Beginnings*, which covers the first five books of the Bible.

By reading the Bible this way, as a narrative rather than a

recipe box, I have been astonished at the ways God speaks to his friends, whether Moses, Abraham, Elijah, David, and Isaiah in the Old Testament, or Peter, Paul, Mary, and John in the New Testament. I'm noticing for the first time how chatty God is with his friends. You never have to initiate a conversation with God. He's the first one to jump in because he loves to talk with us, touch us, and heal us.

May God open our hearts and imaginations to his friendship, believing that the things that happened to our Bible heroes could happen to us.

PRAYER AND THE HEALING POWER OF GOD

Prayer is the most effective way for us to hear God's voice and to feel his touch. Sadly, many of us treat prayer as a one-way conversation. I was raised to understand that prayer is coming to God with my requests. As a kid I remember attending the Wednesday night prayer meeting at our church, where people would make their requests known to God in front of everyone else (usually a small crowd). Mostly the prayers were for people who were sick, and usually the prayers were specific.

"O Lord, we pray for Esther's arthritis, that her pain may go away." Or, "Dear Father, please bring healing to Mr. Johnson, who had a heart attack last week." My dad called these prayer meetings "organ recitals" because people mostly prayed for parts of the body to get better.

I don't mean to disparage the traditional prayer meeting, which has gone by the wayside along with flannelgraph stories and red punch. But as I look back on the times of prayer I experienced in my church, I wonder what God thought about them. In fact, anytime we use prayer as merely a way to get God to take care of business, I imagine him wanting so much more from us because he is so much more than a celestial vending machine. "When you surrender initiative," writes Willard, "you make prayer meaningless. It lifts your spirits but does not influence what God is going to do."[12]

"Prayer is an honest exchange between people who are doing things together," Willard continues. "God and I work together, and I need to invoke his power in that activity. Joint activity is a key to understanding how conversation flows."[13]

When you pray, try picturing yourself in an actual conversation with God. You wouldn't sit down with a friend, give him or her a list of things you want and need, and then say, "Goodbye, let me know when you get everything done." You wouldn't have much of a friendship. Instead, you would have a real give-and-take conversation, sharing things about your life, and then listening to your friend's response.

So how does God respond? How do we hear his voice when we pray? First, we may want to ease back on our own organ recitals. In his excellent little book *Pray Big*, Alistair Begg puts our need to pray for our physical woes in perspective. "Praying for health is almost nonexistent in the Bible, but probably the number one prayer request for Western Christians." Begg says we put a top priority on praying for health and healing because we don't want to die. "We want to live," he continues. "We think life here on earth is way better than what God has for us on the other side of death."[14]

Again, imagine conversing with a friend, and all she talks about is her desire to stay healthy and live a long life. You would be bored in no time. "Tell me something about your dreams and desires, something that matters," you might say. So it is with God. Begg reminds us, "We should be praying less about the practical details of this life and focus more on the spiritual realities of our eternal life. All that matters may be brought before God, but what we bring before God is not always what matters most."[15]

LEARNING TO HEAR GOD'S VOICE

In my view, Dallas Willard's *Hearing God* is the most insightful, practical, and helpful book on hearing God's voice you could read. Here are three characteristics of God's voice suggested by Willard that put us in the best position to hear God's side of our conversations with him. Willard designates these as *quality*, *spirit*, and *content*.[16]

The Quality of God's Voice

Some people claim to have heard God audibly, and I would never dispute that. God spoke audibly to plenty of Bible characters, and he can certainly speak that way today. But for most of us, God's voice will come through "certain thoughts or perceptions that enter our minds." These aren't sounds as such, so when talking about the *quality* of God's voice, Willard is thinking more about "the *weight* or impact an impression makes on our consciousness." When we hear it, says Willard, "our innermost being seems to say, *Yes, this is true and right.*"

The people who listened to Jesus knew that "he taught with real authority—quite unlike their teachers of religious law" (Matthew 7:29). As the Spirit of Jesus speaks to our inner lives, we will also recognize that authority.

The Spirit of God's Voice

This spirit has to do with "exalted peacefulness and confidence, of joy, of sweet reasonableness and of goodwill." If you want a quick reminder of how the Spirit of God speaks to you, review the fruit of the Spirit listed in Galatians 5:22-23. The voice of God "is not the voice of a bully," Willard assures us. "It will not run over you and your will. It is, in short, the spirit of Jesus, and by that phrase I refer to the overall tone and internal dynamics of his personal life as a whole."

The Content of God's Voice

What God says to your inner spirit will never contradict what God has said in his Word. "Any content or claim that does not conform to biblical content is not a word from God. Period!" This is why it is so important for the growing Christian to be a diligent student of the Scriptures. As the apostle Paul taught his student, Timothy,

> Work hard so you can present yourself to God and receive his approval. Be a good worker, one who does not need to be ashamed and who correctly explains the word of truth (2 Timothy 2:15).

One of the supernatural benefits of hearing God's voice through the lens of Scripture is that it will speak to you long after you have stopped reading it. There is a residual effect that extends through the day and night as the Holy Spirit brings God's truth to mind when you need it most. I have found that there's something restful and reassuring about reading from the Bible right before I go to bed. His voice seems to seep into my subconscious even as I sleep.

> I will bless the LORD who guides me;
> even at night my heart instructs me.
>   (Psalm 16:7)

BECOMING NATURALLY SUPERNATURAL

Throughout this book, I have confessed to you that I have lived most of my life as if the natural world is all that exists. Oh, I have always believed in the supernatural world that God inhabits. My confidence in the world to come, where I will live with Jesus in heaven after my life on earth is done, has never wavered. But my focus has been natural rather than supernatural.

All that has changed.

The research, reading, praying, and writing that went into this book—not to mention the surprising voice of God that is permeating my life—have combined to amplify my belief in the supernatural and the healing power of God. I'm not there yet—far from it—but I am in the process of becoming naturally supernatural.

I first heard that phrase from my friend J.P. Moreland, distinguished professor of philosophy at Biola University's Talbot School of Theology. J.P. is a committed Christian and one of the most brilliant people on the planet. He is also a firm practitioner of the supernatural life. In his book *Kingdom Triangle*, Moreland writes,

> While I still have much to learn about the Kingdom's supernatural power, I have changed dramatically in recent years regarding what I have seen, heard, and done. I began as a cessationist, lived for years as an open but cautious Evangelical, and would now be considered a Third Wave Evangelical.[17]

Moreland suggests that anyone who desires to be more "naturally supernatural" should keep three things in mind:[18]

- Never force it. Living in the reality of the

supernatural must be authentic and consistent with "the nature of God's Kingdom."

- Be gentle, humble, and patient with yourself and others "as you grow in the miraculous." At the end of the day, our journey to embrace the supernatural is not about us. "It's about becoming more effective colaborers with God in the Great Commission enterprise."

- Don't try to "create faith by simply trying directly to believe something more strongly than you do." Genuine faith grows by study, meditation, risk, and learning from your successes and failures.

Whether you have been a Christian for years or you're just starting out, now is the time to become naturally supernatural. It isn't necessary to change churches, and you don't need years of study before you can embrace the supernatural life God wants you to enjoy. You can begin right now.

CHAPTER 7

A Biblical Embrace of the Supernatural...Today

A 30-Day Devotional Journey

There is more to the supernatural than healing, such as the unseen world of angels, Satan, and demons. But unlike those very real manifestations, the healing power of God goes directly to the heart of who God is and why he sent Jesus to sacrifice his life so that we could experience his healing power, both physically and spiritually.

In your desire to know more about the healing power of God, I hope that your view of your life in Christ has been expanded to include the supernatural qualities that give your life power and meaning. There is a practical side to the Christian life, but without the supernatural, Christianity is no better than any other man-made religion.

To help you embrace your supernatural life, I have created a 30-day devotional journey, drawing on twelve miracles in the Old Testament, and eighteen miracles in the New Testament. Each day you can read about a miracle, and then reflect on what it means to you personally and practically as you embrace—by God's grace and in his power—the supernatural.

Come and see what our God has done,
what awesome miracles he performs for people!

Psalm 66:5

DAY 1

The Stairway to Heaven

GENESIS 28:10-17

Meanwhile, Jacob left Beersheba and traveled toward Haran. At sundown he arrived at a good place to set up camp and stopped there for the night. Jacob found a stone to rest his head against and lay down to sleep. As he slept, he dreamed of a stairway that reached from the earth up to heaven. And he saw the angels of God going up and down the stairway.

At the top of the stairway stood the LORD, and he said, "I am the LORD, the God of your grandfather Abraham, and the God of your father, Isaac. The ground you are lying on belongs to you. I am giving it to you and your descendants. Your descendants will be as numerous as the dust of the earth! They will spread out in all directions—to the west and the east, to the north and the south. And all the families of the earth will be blessed through you and your descendants. What's more, I am with you, and I will protect you wherever you go. One day I will bring you back to this land. I will not leave you until I have finished giving you everything I have promised you."

Then Jacob awoke from his sleep and said, "Surely the LORD is in this place, and I wasn't even aware of it!" But he was also afraid and said, "What an awesome place this is! It is none other than the house of God, the very gateway to heaven!"

THE LIMINAL SPACE BETWEEN HEAVEN AND EARTH

What is it like to catch a glimpse of the threshold between heaven and earth? Jacob's dream infuses our imagination with glorious snapshots of this unseen yet fully formed world. The "stairway to heaven" has inspired art and memorable music. But oils and notes are unable to capture the true splendor of this space.

Jacob did his best to describe the wonders of his dream. Imagine! He saw God standing at the top of the stairway. The Lord Almighty taking a form Jacob would understand and relate to. God's angels alighting along this celestial pathway. This majestic Creator is the God of his father and grandfather. How Jacob's heart must have been stirred in his twilight of sleep. He saw God's house! He gazed upon the very gateway to heaven!

Have you ever awakened from a splendid dream, saddened that you had to leave that place and return to your normal state? Imagine how Jacob felt when he woke from this vivid revelation. While we are on earth, there are many wonders to behold and beautiful vistas to experience. But someday we will permanently dwell in that place that is perceptible only in that space between the natural and supernatural.

A BIBLICAL EMBRACE OF THE SUPERNATURAL...TODAY

We can't live there now, but we can imagine what it will be like, when the liminal space between heaven and earth will be our glorious dwelling in the presence of the Lord our God.

DAY 2

The Burning Bush

Exodus 3:1-6

One day Moses was tending the flock of his father-in-law, Jethro, the priest of Midian. He led the flock far into the wilderness and came to Sinai, the mountain of God. There the angel of the LORD appeared to him in a blazing fire from the middle of a bush. Moses stared in amazement. Though the bush was engulfed in flames, it didn't burn up. "This is amazing," Moses said to himself. "Why isn't that bush burning up? I must go see it."

When the LORD saw Moses coming to take a closer look, God called to him from the middle of the bush, "Moses! Moses!"

"Here I am!" Moses replied.

"Do not come any closer," the LORD warned. "Take off your sandals, for you are standing on holy ground. I am the God of your father—the God of Abraham, the God of Isaac, and the God of Jacob." When Moses heard this, he covered his face because he was afraid to look at God.

YOU ARE STANDING ON
HOLY GROUND

I often long to be in the place where God's presence fills me, but sometimes the experience comes with a price. After pondering the story of Moses' encounter with the burning bush in the desert, I understand why.

The miracle of a bush burning but not consumed is in itself a supernatural wonder. Moses is amazed. But as he approaches the phenomenon to get a closer look, God calls his name twice and tells him to stop because he is standing on holy ground.

In my desire to be in God's supernatural presence, I have been entirely too casual. This business of taking off your shoes seems simple enough. I can do that out of reverence and respect. But that's not what is happening here, and Moses' response gives us a clue. After God instructs Moses on his footwear removal, he is afraid to look at God. Why? Because in those days in that part of the world the only reason to take off one's sandals was not to offer respect, but to confess unworthiness. Moses is afraid because he realizes he is in the presence of almighty, all-holy, all-powerful God.

A BIBLICAL EMBRACE OF
THE SUPERNATURAL...TODAY

When we encounter the supernatural manifestation of God in any form, may we remember how unworthy we are, and how gracious God is to allow us to enter his holy presence.

DAY 3

Manna from Heaven

EXODUS 16:11-18

The LORD said to Moses, "I have heard the Israelites' complaints. Now tell them, 'In the evening you will have meat to eat, and in the morning you will have all the bread you want. Then you will know that I am the LORD your God.'"

That evening vast numbers of quail flew in and covered the camp. And the next morning the area around the camp was wet with dew. When the dew evaporated, a flaky substance as fine as frost blanketed the ground. The Israelites were puzzled when they saw it. "What is it?" they asked each other. They had no idea what it was.

And Moses told them, "It is the food the LORD has given you to eat. These are the LORD's instructions: Each household should gather as much as it needs. Pick up two quarts for each person in your tent."

So the people of Israel did as they were told. Some gathered a lot, some only a little. But when they measured it out, everyone had just enough. Those who gathered a lot had nothing left over, and those who gathered only a little had enough. Each family had just what it needed.

THE MIRACLE OF
GOD'S PROVISION

What is a provision? It's a rather antiquated term that describes meeting a need. In days gone by, people would speak of getting provisions for a journey. Because weight mattered, excess was unthinkable. You secured just enough food and water to get you to your destination, where there would be more provisions. When it comes to our earthly provisions, we have come to expect abundance. "Just enough" doesn't occur to us because, well, what if we run out? How will we eat? So we store up more than we need. Just enough isn't enough.

Have you ever prayed for God to supply your needs, and he does just that, but not in abundance? You may feel a tinge of disappointment, but this is God's way. He hasn't promised us a life free of struggle and pain, but he assures us that in our want and pain and suffering, he will provide what we need at the time we need it.

The healing power of God isn't like a magic wand waved around by an imaginary fairy, making everything right again. God's power is personal and specific. We don't need to store his blessings for tomorrow, for he has given us everything we need today to satisfy our physical, emotional, and spiritual needs.

A BIBLICAL EMBRACE OF
THE SUPERNATURAL...TODAY

The faithful love of the LORD never ends! His mercies never cease. Great is his faithfulness; his mercies begin afresh each morning (Lamentations 3:22-23).

DAY 4

Gideon's Fleece

JUDGES 6:33-40

Soon afterward the armies of Midian, Amalek, and the people of the east formed an alliance against Israel and crossed the Jordan, camping in the valley of Jezreel. Then the Spirit of the LORD clothed Gideon with power. He blew a ram's horn as a call to arms, and the men of the clan of Abiezer came to him. He also sent messengers throughout Manasseh, Asher, Zebulun, and Naphtali, summoning their warriors, and all of them responded.

Then Gideon said to God, "If you are truly going to use me to rescue Israel as you promised, prove it to me in this way. I will put a wool fleece on the threshing floor tonight. If the fleece is wet with dew in the morning but the ground is dry, then I will know that you are going to help me rescue Israel as you promised." And that is just what happened. When Gideon got up early the next morning, he squeezed the fleece and wrung out a whole bowlful of water.

Then Gideon said to God, "Please don't be angry with me, but let me make one more request. Let me use the fleece for one more test. This time let the fleece remain dry while the ground around it is wet with dew." So that night God did as Gideon asked. The fleece was dry in the morning, but the ground was covered with dew.

GOD UNDERSTANDS
OUR DOUBTS

Gideon is a mighty warrior God chooses to fight for his people against their enemies. The first order of business for Gideon is to destroy the altars built to the pagan gods. He quickly takes care of this, causing several opposing nations to take up arms against Israel. In order to equip him with the skill and courage needed for battle, the Spirit of the Lord supernaturally covers Gideon. It should be all Gideon needs to meet the challenge ahead, but he wants assurance.

Specifically, Gideon wants a sign that he will be successful. So he puts out a fleece and asks God to make it wet while keeping the ground around it dry, which God does. The next night, just to be absolutely sure, Gideon asks God to reverse the effect. God patiently does as Gideon requests.

We can roll our eyes at this need for double assurance, but don't we do the same thing? We even call it "putting out a fleece." If there's any eye-rolling going on, it should be God rolling his eyes at us when we don't trust him. He has clothed us with every spiritual blessing, yet we want more. Give Gideon credit for self-awareness. He guesses God might be angry with him for doubting, but he guesses wrong. God condescends and agrees to answer Gideon at his point of need.

A BIBLICAL EMBRACE OF
THE SUPERNATURAL...TODAY

We may at times fail to trust God, but he understands. Just as his compassion is never ending, so is his forbearance. Just as his love for us endures, so does his patience.

God Calls Samuel... Three Times

1 Samuel 3:2-10

One night Eli, who was almost blind by now, had gone to bed. The lamp of God had not yet gone out, and Samuel was sleeping in the Tabernacle near the Ark of God. Suddenly the Lord called out, "Samuel!"

"Yes?" Samuel replied. "What is it?" He got up and ran to Eli. "Here I am. Did you call me?"

"I didn't call you," Eli replied. "Go back to bed." So he did. Then the Lord called out again, "Samuel!"

Again Samuel got up and went to Eli. "Here I am. Did you call me?"

"I didn't call you, my son," Eli said. "Go back to bed."

Samuel did not yet know the Lord because he had never had a message from the Lord before. So the Lord called a third time, and once more Samuel got up and went to Eli. "Here I am. Did you call me?"

Then Eli realized it was the Lord who was calling the boy. So he said to Samuel, "Go and lie down again, and if someone calls again, say, 'Speak, Lord, your servant is listening.'" So Samuel went back to bed. And the Lord came and called as before, "Samuel! Samuel!"

And Samuel replied, "Speak, your servant is listening."

LISTEN TO GOD'S VOICE

Four times in the Old Testament, God calls someone by saying their name twice, each time for something beyond that person's ability to handle. That's how the supernatural call of God works. When God wants something done, he will ask someone quite ordinary to do it.

Samuel is but a boy, yet God has his hand on him. Logic dictates that Eli should be chosen to hear God's voice. He is the priest and has the experience, but his time has passed. Yet Samuel respects Eli and defers to him each time he hears the voice of God. For his part, Eli may have made mistakes in his life, but he does the right thing by helping Samuel understand that it is God who is calling his name.

Credit Eli for taking on the role of encourager for the next generation, the next leader, the one who will take his place. This is what capable leaders do, especially those who are sensitive to God's voice. If you are in a place to help and inspire those younger than you, let this little story of the supernatural voice of God be your guide.

And if you are young and are hearing God call you, respond the way Samuel does: "Speak, your servant is listening."

A BIBLICAL EMBRACE OF
THE SUPERNATURAL...TODAY

Living a supernatural life means receiving God's direction, whether the Spirit of God speaks to our inner being or the voice of God is as clear to us as it was to Samuel.

DAY 6

Elijah Heals
the Widow's Son

1 KINGS 17:17-24

Some time later the woman's son became sick. He grew worse and worse, and finally he died. Then she said to Elijah, "O man of God, what have you done to me? Have you come here to point out my sins and kill my son?"

But Elijah replied, "Give me your son." And he took the child's body from her arms, carried him up the stairs to the room where he was staying, and laid the body on his bed. Then Elijah cried out to the LORD, "O LORD my God, why have you brought tragedy to this widow who has opened her home to me, causing her son to die?"

And he stretched himself out over the child three times and cried out to the LORD, "O LORD my God, please let this child's life return to him." The LORD heard Elijah's prayer, and the life of the child returned, and he revived! Then Elijah brought him down from the upper room and gave him to his mother. "Look!" he said. "Your son is alive!"

Then the woman told Elijah, "Now I know for sure that you are a man of God, and that the LORD truly speaks through you."

"OH DEATH,
WHERE IS YOUR VICTORY?"

This is the first of three cases in the Bible when the son of a widow dies and is then restored to life. Elisha also raises a widow's son (2 Kings 8), as does Jesus (Luke 7). In this case, the widow is not just stricken by grief, but confused and angry, so she turns her indignation to Elijah. In response to the widow's accusations, Elijah turns the indignation to God. This has become a personal matter.

Perhaps that's why this resurrection is so physical. Elijah stretches his own body over the child three times, crying out to the Lord each time. God hears and answers Elijah's impassioned prayers and brings the boy back to life. "Now I know," the widow exclaims, her heart exultant. She knows that Elijah truly is a prophet of God. She understands the reality of *Jehovah Rophe*, the God who heals.

As Elijah did before him, Jesus demonstrates indignation when his friend Lazarus dies (John 11:33-39). But he doesn't blame his Father. Instead, Jesus turns his sorrow and anger to death itself, ultimately defeating the last enemy by his own death on the cross and his resurrection after three days in the tomb.

A BIBLICAL EMBRACE OF
THE SUPERNATURAL...TODAY

When we put Elijah's story of healing in the context of what Jesus did, we can agree with the apostle Paul: "O death, where is your victory? Oh death, where is your sting?" (1 Corinthians 15:55).

DAY 7

The Voice of God

1 Kings 19:7-13

The angel of the Lord came again and touched him and said, "Get up and eat some more, or the journey ahead will be too much for you." So he got up and ate and drank, and the food gave him enough strength to travel forty days and forty nights to Mount Sinai, the mountain of God. There he came to a cave, where he spent the night.

But the Lord said to him, "What are you doing here, Elijah?"

Elijah replied, "I have zealously served the Lord God Almighty. But the people of Israel have broken their covenant with you, torn down your altars, and killed every one of your prophets. I am the only one left, and now they are trying to kill me, too."

"Go out and stand before me on the mountain," the Lord told him. And as Elijah stood there, the Lord passed by, and a mighty windstorm hit the mountain. It was such a terrible blast that the rocks were torn loose, but the Lord was not in the wind. After the wind there was an earthquake, but the Lord was not in the earthquake. And after the earthquake there was a fire, but the Lord was not in the fire. And after the fire there was the sound of a gentle whisper. When Elijah heard it, he wrapped his face in his cloak and went out and stood at the entrance of the cave.

And a voice said, "What are you doing here, Elijah?"

BE STILL AND LISTEN

Elijah was a fiery prophet usually given to excess and emotion, but on this occasion Elijah's emotions are on the other side of the spectrum. Having fled for his life from King Ahab, he is afraid and discouraged. An angel ministers to Elijah, giving him food for a 40-day journey. Elijah reaches Sinai, the mountain of God, where he spends the night in a cave.

When God tells Elijah to stand before him on the mountain, Elijah probably expects God to come at him through some kind of dramatic expression of the natural world. But God isn't in any of those elements. Instead, he shows up in a whisper.

Sometimes our lives become so frenzied and cacophonous that we think the only way to hear God's voice is through something extravagant. When we pray, we want God to answer dramatically. If we pray for someone to be healed, we expect an immediate miracle. But that's not God's way. "Gracious souls are more affected by the tender mercies of the Lord than by his terrors," writes Matthew Henry.[1] It's not nature's drama, but the still voice of God that causes Elijah to cover his face, for he knows God has answered.

A BIBLICAL EMBRACE OF
THE SUPERNATURAL...TODAY

Our prayers—for guidance, for provision, for healing— should be bold. And when we have prayed, we should be still and listen for God to speak.

DAY 8

Naaman Is Healed of Leprosy

2 Kings 5:2-3; 9-14

Though Naaman was a mighty warrior, he suffered from leprosy.

At this time Aramean raiders had invaded the land of Israel, and among their captives was a young girl who had been given to Naaman's wife as a maid. One day the girl said to her mistress, "I wish my master would go to see the prophet in Samaria. He would heal him of his leprosy."...

So Naaman went with his horses and chariots and waited at the door of Elisha's house. But Elisha sent a messenger out to him with this message: "Go and wash yourself seven times in the Jordan River. Then your skin will be restored, and you will be healed of your leprosy."

But Naaman became angry and stalked away. "I thought he would certainly come out to meet me!" he said. "I expected him to wave his hand over the leprosy and call on the name of the Lord his God and heal me! So Naaman turned and went away in a rage.

But his officers tried to reason with him and said, "Sir, if the prophet had told you to do something very difficult, wouldn't you have done it? So you should certainly obey him when he says simply, 'Go and wash and be cured!'" So Naaman went down to the Jordan River and dipped himself seven times, as the man of God had instructed him. And his skin became as healthy as the skin of a young child, and he was healed!

WE DON'T GET TO
SET THE TERMS

Naaman represents so much that is wrong with us when we get a little success under our belt. Having achieved a status admired by many, he has become proud. And yet despite his social standing. Naaman has leprosy, reminding us that disease is no respecter of persons—rich or poor, strong or weak.

Does Elisha know Naaman is a proud man? Seems that way. Otherwise, why wouldn't he do what Naaman expected: meet him in person, wave a hand, and swoosh, no more leprosy!? But that's not how God or his prophets do things, especially when pride is center stage. For healing to take place, there must be submission to God's way and God's time. And we must be alert to the ways he works, which are sometimes unconventional. It's not that God doesn't want to heal Naaman. Clearly he does, but he uses people on the other end of the social ladder—his wife's maid, Naaman's direct reports—to guide him to his healing.

There's another lesson tucked into this marvelous story. Matthew Henry observes that leprosy represents the sin in all of our lives.[2] It's pervasive and deadly. God longs to give us spiritual healing, but we can't experience God's touch if we want it done our way. We must surrender and be washed in the life-giving water of the Spirit and the precious blood of Jesus.

A BIBLICAL EMBRACE OF
THE SUPERNATURAL...TODAY

Oh, that we would keep the eyes of our heart open to God's voice and the often unusual ways he speaks to us.

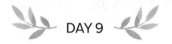

DAY 9

Open His Eyes
and Let Him See!

2 Kings 6:10-17

The king of Israel would send word to the place indicated by the man of God. Time and again Elisha warned the king, so that he would be on the alert there.

The king of Aram became very upset over this. He called his officers together and demanded, "Which of you is the traitor? Who has been informing the king of Israel of my plans?"

"It's not us, my lord the king," one of the officers replied. "Elisha, the prophet in Israel, tells the king of Israel even the words you speak in the privacy of your bedroom!"

"Go and find out where he is," the king commanded, "so I can send troops to seize him." And the report came back: "Elisha is at Dothan." So one night the king of Aram sent a great army with many chariots and horses to surround the city.

When the servant of the man of God got up early the next morning and went outside, there were troops, horses, and chariots everywhere. "Oh, sir, what will we do now?" the young man cried to Elisha.

"Don't be afraid!" Elisha told him. "For there are more on our side than on theirs!" Then Elisha prayed, "O Lord, open his eyes and let him see!" The Lord opened the young man's eyes, and when he looked up, he saw that the hillside around Elisha was filled with horses and chariots of fire.

OPENING THE EYES
OF FAITH

Few would argue that the spirit of this world is a spirit of fear. There is always something to be afraid of. If it's not the conflict we see between nations, we fear some kind of virus or a pending natural disaster. Or an illness that threatens us or someone we love. Even the prospect of losing a job can produce fear.

Elijah's servant has good reason to be afraid. Imagine waking up from a deep sleep only to see that you're surrounded by soldiers and their implements of war, poised to capture you. Fearing for your life would be a natural and appropriate response. Elijah's response confronts his servant's fear head on: "Don't be afraid!" These aren't empty words, but true to the reality of the supernatural world. Those who trust God have more on their side than the enemy has on his side. "Greater is he who is in you than he who is in the world," the apostle Paul confirms (1 John 4:4 NASB).

Too often when confronted with a situation that causes us to fear, we are like Elijah's servant—with an eye on earthly things—when we should emulate Elijah, whose eyes saw the supernatural reality around him.

A BIBLICAL EMBRACE OF
THE SUPERNATURAL...TODAY

Embracing a supernatural life means opening the eyes of faith to see the reality of God's divine presence and protection.

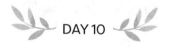

DAY 10

King Hezekiah
Asks for Healing

2 KINGS 20:1-6

About that time Hezekiah became deathly ill, and the prophet Isaiah son of Amoz went to visit him. He gave the king this message: "This is what the LORD says: Set your affairs in order, for you are going to die. You will not recover from this illness."

When Hezekiah heard this, he turned his face to the wall and prayed to the LORD, "Remember, O LORD, how I have always been faithful to you and have served you single-mindedly, always doing what pleases you." Then he broke down and wept bitterly.

But before Isaiah had left the middle courtyard, this message came to him from the LORD: "Go back to Hezekiah, the leader of my people. Tell him, 'This is what the LORD, the God of your ancestor David, says: I have heard your prayer and seen your tears. I will heal you, and three days from now you will get out of bed and go to the Temple of the LORD. I will add fifteen years to your life, and I will rescue you and this city from the king of Assyria. I will defend this city for my own honor and for the sake of my servant David.'"

THE LORD IS CLOSE TO THE BROKENHEARTED

I have never met someone who wanted to die. Everyone I know wants to live longer. For many, the desire to cling to life is the fear of loss. For others, it's the unknown. Even those who firmly believe they will be with Jesus in heaven when they die don't relish the prospect of death. That's why Christians want so badly to believe God heals today like he did in Bible times. Yes, we want God's healing power, but most of the time we just want to live longer.

You know, there's nothing wrong with that, and here's why. Hezekiah is a good king with unfinished business. When God tells him he is going to die, he is distressed. How could he die now when there is so much good he can still do for God's people? In his grief, Hezekiah turns his face to the wall and prays earnestly and with tears, asking God to heal him. And God is moved.

God's response is tender and should give us hope: "I have heard your prayer and seen your tears." God is compassionate and cares about us and our suffering. As the psalmist David writes, "The LORD is close to the brokenhearted; he rescues those whose spirits are crushed" (Psalm 34:18).

A BIBLICAL EMBRACE OF
THE SUPERNATURAL...TODAY

In Scripture, healing *and* saves *come from the same root word. Sometimes we experience God's healing, but can always have confidence in his willingness and ability to save.*

Daniel in the Lion's Den

DANIEL 6:16-23

At last the king gave orders for Daniel to be arrested and thrown into the den of lions. The king said to him, "May your God, whom you serve so faithfully, rescue you."

A stone was brought and placed over the mouth of the den. The king sealed the stone with his own royal seal and the seals of his nobles, so that no one could rescue Daniel. Then the king returned to his palace and spent the night fasting. He refused his usual entertainment and couldn't sleep at all that night.

Very early the next morning, the king got up and hurried out to the lions' den. When he got there, he called out in anguish, "Daniel, servant of the living God! Was your God, whom you serve so faithfully, able to rescue you from the lions?"

Daniel answered, "Long live the king! My God sent his angel to shut the lions' mouths so that they would not hurt me, for I have been found innocent in his sight. And I have not wronged you, Your Majesty."

The king was overjoyed and ordered that Daniel be lifted from the den. Not a scratch was found on him, for he had trusted in his God.

MORE TO THE STORY

What can we learn from one of the most familiar stories in the Bible? When I first heard the story of Daniel in the lion's den in Sunday school, I thought it meant I was to have courage and trust God to protect me. Those takeaways are true, but there's more to the story if you view it in light of the supernatural.

The king, entrapped by Daniel's enemies to dispose of him, wants Daniel to be saved. He probably remembers that God miraculously delivered Daniel's friends after they were thrown into the fiery furnace (Daniel 3), so he hopes for such a rescue now. And then, as if he wants to be sure that it will take a miracle to save Daniel, the king orders a stone placed over the den's mouth and seals it, reminding us of the stone and seal placed on Christ's tomb (Matthew 27:66).

And so it happens. God summons an angel to restrain the hungry lions and protect his servant Daniel, just as God will raise Jesus from the dead and dispatch an angel to roll away the stone.

A BIBLICAL EMBRACE OF
THE SUPERNATURAL...TODAY

Daniel faced the lions because of his loyalty and service to God. When we remain loyal to the King of kings and serve him without question, we can expect to face spiritual opposition, especially from the roaring lion prowling around, seeking someone to devour (1 Peter 5:8).

Jonah and the Fish

JONAH 1:17; 2:3-10

Now the LORD had arranged for a great fish to swallow Jonah. And Jonah was inside the fish for three days and three nights...Then Jonah prayed to the Lord his God from inside the fish. He said...

"You threw me into the ocean depths,
  and I sank down to the heart of the sea.
The mighty waters engulfed me;
  I was buried beneath your wild and stormy waves.
Then I said, 'O LORD, you have driven me from your presence.
  Yet I will look once more toward your holy Temple.'
"I sank beneath the waves, and the waters closed over me.
  Seaweed wrapped itself around my head.
I sank down to the very roots of the mountains.
  I was imprisoned in the earth,
  whose gates lock shut forever.
But you, O LORD my God, snatched me from the jaws of death! As my life was slipping away, I remembered the LORD. And my earnest prayer went out to you in your holy Temple.
Those who worship false gods turn their backs on all God's mercies. But I will offer sacrifices to you with songs of praise, and I will fulfill all my vows.
  For my salvation comes from the LORD alone."

Then the LORD ordered the fish to spit Jonah out onto the beach.

GOD AND THE ANIMALS

Two of the most famous miracles in the Bible involve animals. God holds back the deadly jaws and claws of the lions to protect Daniel, and in the story of Jonah he uses a great fish to deal with the rebellious prophet. As supernatural people living in a supernatural world, God's interaction with animals should not surprise us. In fact, we should be delighted.

Jonah is no innocent victim here. He has offended God, but God is merciful. He saves Jonah physically (from the sea) and spiritually (from himself). Yet to embrace God's salvation, Jonah first has to go through a miraculous and no doubt terrifying experience. If ever there is an example for us to pray in all circumstances, this is it. As Matthew Henry observes, "No place is too strange, and no time is too late to pray."[3]

Jonah's story is also a lesson on how God treats those who have strayed away. He is merciful, compassionate, and forgiving—if the prodigal is willing to come to him in repentance. We know Jonah's repentance is sincere when he begins praying and praising God even before he is rescued. He recognizes that those who turn their backs to God also turn their backs to his mercies.

A BIBLICAL EMBRACE OF
THE SUPERNATURAL...TODAY

The miracle of Jonah being rescued from death after three days in the belly of the fish foreshadows the death and miraculous resurrection of Christ after three days (Matthew 12:40).

DAY 13

Jesus Heals the Blind

MATTHEW 9:27-34

After Jesus left the girl's home, two blind men followed along behind him, shouting, "Son of David, have mercy on us!"

They went right into the house where he was staying, and Jesus asked them, "Do you believe I can make you see?"

"Yes, Lord," they told him, "we do."

Then he touched their eyes and said, "Because of your faith, it will happen." Then their eyes were opened, and they could see! Jesus sternly warned them, "Don't tell anyone about this." But instead, they went out and spread his fame all over the region.

When they left, a demon-possessed man who couldn't speak was brought to Jesus. So Jesus cast out the demon, and then the man began to speak. The crowds were amazed. "Nothing like this has ever happened in Israel!" they exclaimed.

But the Pharisees said, "He can cast out demons because he is empowered by the prince of demons."

"DO YOU BELIEVE?"

Of all the stories of miracles and healing we are looking at in our 30-day biblical embrace of the supernatural, this is the only one where Jesus asks those wanting to be healed, "Do you believe I can heal you?" The response of the blind men shows the depth of their faith.

First, they call him by his messianic name, "Son of David." Theirs is a knowledgeable faith. Then they boldly follow Jesus into the house where he is staying. Theirs is a persistent faith. And when Jesus asks them, "Do you believe I can make you see?" they do more than say, "Yes, Lord, we do." The blind men demonstrate a faith rooted in the power of God to heal, not their own ability. Faith like this understands that there is no limit to what Jesus will do for those who believe, if they will just trust him.

Immediately after healing the eyes of the two blind men so they could see, Jesus casts a demon out of a man so he could speak. Unlike the two blind men, the Pharisees are clueless because they don't accept that Jesus is the Messiah sent by God. If they had, they would have known Jesus was fulfilling the prophecy of Isaiah concerning the One who will open the eyes of the blind and cause those who cannot speak to sing for joy (Isaiah 35:5-6).

A BIBLICAL EMBRACE OF
THE SUPERNATURAL...TODAY

Jesus tells the two blind men not to tell anyone about their healing. But like anyone who has felt the supernatural touch of God, they can't help but tell everyone.

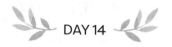

Jesus Heals a Demon Possessed Boy

Matthew 17:14-20

At the foot of the mountain, a large crowd was waiting for them. A man came and knelt before Jesus and said, "Lord, have mercy on my son. He has seizures and suffers terribly. He often falls into the fire or into the water. So I brought him to your disciples, but they couldn't heal him."

Jesus said, "You faithless and corrupt people! How long must I be with you? How long must I put up with you? Bring the boy here to me." Then Jesus rebuked the demon in the boy, and it left him. From that moment the boy was well.

Afterward the disciples asked Jesus privately, "Why couldn't we cast out that demon?"

"You don't have enough faith," Jesus told them. "I tell you the truth, if you had faith even as small as a mustard seed, you could say to this mountain, 'Move from here to there,' and it would move. Nothing would be impossible."

NOTHING IS IMPOSSIBLE

Faith can be a tricky thing. Most of us don't have any trouble believing in God, that he exists and created the world and sent Jesus to earth to give us eternal life if we put our trust in him. But when it comes to believing God that everything he has told us in his Word and through the Holy Spirit is true, well, that's where our faith sometimes comes up short.

The disciples believe *in* Jesus, but they don't *believe* Jesus— at least not yet. If they did, they would remember when he first sent them out and told them, "Heal the sick, raise the dead, cure those with leprosy, and cast out demons. Give as freely as you have received!" (Matthew 10:8). Jesus has already given the disciples authority to cast out demons, but they don't believe it is possible. That's why he responds the way he does. When we fail to trust Jesus completely, he grieves over our unbelief.

Whatever the task in front of you, *believing in* Jesus isn't enough. You need to *believe* Jesus and put your faith into action by trusting that his supernatural power can overcome anything, even the dark powers of this world.

A BIBLICAL EMBRACE OF
THE SUPERNATURAL...TODAY

When you are open to the power of God in your life, even if the task seems impossible, it is like you are opening a curtain so the healing light of Jesus can come in.

Jesus Heals a Woman Bleeding for Twelve Years

MARK 5:27-34

Jesus went with him, and all the people followed, crowding around him. A woman in the crowd had suffered for twelve years with constant bleeding. She had suffered a great deal from many doctors, and over the years she had spent everything she had to pay them, but she had gotten no better. In fact, she had gotten worse. She had heard about Jesus, so she came up behind him through the crowd and touched his robe. For she thought to herself, "If I can just touch his robe, I will be healed." Immediately the bleeding stopped, and she could feel in her body that she had been healed of her terrible condition.

Jesus realized at once that healing power had gone out from him, so he turned around in the crowd and asked, "Who touched my robe?"

His disciples said to him, "Look at this crowd pressing around you. How can you ask, 'Who touched me?'"

But he kept on looking around to see who had done it. Then the frightened woman, trembling at the realization of what had happened to her, came and fell to her knees in front of him and told him what she had done. And he said to her, "Daughter, your faith has made you well. Go in peace. Your suffering is over."

A FAITH THAT SAVES

Here is an example of "faith even as small as a mustard seed." The woman in this story is ceremonially unclean, meaning she is being shunned. Most likely she's embarrassed and doesn't want to be noticed by Jesus or the crowd. But such is her faith that she believes Jesus can heal her just by touching the edge of his robe. And that's exactly what happens! The woman's faith may be small, but it is effective because she doesn't just believe in Jesus. She believes Jesus can heal her with just the slightest touch.

The woman tries to slip into the crowd, but Jesus wants to know how it was that his healing power "had gone out from him." This is one of those cases where the humanity of Jesus is on full display. Because he is fully God and fully human, Jesus can sympathize with our weakness. He knows what it's like to suffer.

When the woman finally comes forward, her healing is complete. Not only is her suffering over, but she has also experienced a spiritual transformation. The sentence "Your faith has made you well" literally means "Your faith has saved you." Jesus sometimes brings physical healing to those with broken bodies, but he always saves those who call on him by faith.

A BIBLICAL EMBRACE OF
THE SUPERNATURAL...TODAY

Crowds may throng around Jesus, but only those who trust him and reach out to touch him by faith will experience his supernatural healing touch.

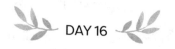

Jesus Raises Jairus' Daughter

Mark 5:35-43

While he was still speaking to her, messengers arrived from the home of Jairus, the leader of the synagogue. They told him, "Your daughter is dead. There's no use troubling the Teacher now."

But Jesus overheard them and said to Jairus, "Don't be afraid. Just have faith."

Then Jesus stopped the crowd and wouldn't let anyone go with him except Peter, James, and John (the brother of James). When they came to the home of the synagogue leader, Jesus saw much commotion and weeping and wailing. He went inside and asked, "Why all this commotion and weeping? The child isn't dead; she's only asleep."

The crowd laughed at him. But he made them all leave, and he took the girl's father and mother and his three disciples into the room where the girl was lying. Holding her hand, he said to her, "Talitha koum," which means "Little girl, get up!" And the girl, who was twelve years old, immediately stood up and walked around! They were overwhelmed and totally amazed. Jesus gave them strict orders not to tell anyone what had happened, and then he told them to give her something to eat.

"DON'T BE AFRAID. JUST HAVE FAITH."

Immediately after healing a woman, Jesus is told the daughter of Jairus has died. Earlier in this story, the little girl was "at the point of death" (Mark 5:23 NASB). But Jesus is sidetracked by the crowd following him and the woman who touches the edge of his robe. Of course, that's not completely accurate. Jesus is never sidetracked or distracted. He is always purposeful and ready to meet us at our point of need.

Yet we fear. We fear the circumstances threatening to overwhelm us. We fear the uncertainty of the world around us. We especially fear death. But those who know Jesus have nothing to fear, as this story of Jesus illustrates. In the presence of Jesus, the Lord of life, death is but a temporary condition. Death may bring sorrow to loved ones, but those who have faith in Jesus know that death is nothing to fear.

The world doesn't get this. When Jesus says, "The child isn't dead; she's only asleep," people laugh. So he makes them leave, taking just the girl's parents and three disciples into the room to witness the resurrection. Then, simply by a word of power, Jesus restores her life. So it is with us. It is by the word of Christ that supernatural life is given.

A BIBLICAL EMBRACE OF THE SUPERNATURAL...TODAY

Those in the room are "overwhelmed and totally amazed." As we see God work supernaturally in our lives, we should never be surprised, but always amazed.

Blind Bartimaeus
Throws Off His Cloak

MARK 10:46-52

They reached Jericho, and as Jesus and his disciples left town, a large crowd followed him. A blind beggar named Bartimaeus (son of Timaeus) was sitting beside the road. When Bartimaeus heard that Jesus of Nazareth was nearby, he began to shout, "Jesus, Son of David, have mercy on me!"

"Be quiet!" many of the people yelled at him. But he only shouted louder, "Son of David, have mercy on me!"

When Jesus heard him, he stopped and said, "Tell him to come here." So they called the blind man. "Cheer up," they said. "Come on, he's calling you!" Bartimaeus threw aside his coat, jumped up, and came to Jesus.

"What do you want me to do for you?" Jesus asked.

"My Rabbi," the blind man said, "I want to see!"

And Jesus said to him, "Go, for your faith has healed you." Instantly the man could see, and he followed Jesus down the road.

ABANDONING ALL
TO FOLLOW JESUS

Like the blind men in Matthew 9, Bartimaeus calls Jesus by his messianic title, also aware of the prophecy concerning his healing power (Isaiah 35:5-6). When Jesus hears Bartimaeus call his name, he stops. Jesus always has time for suffering individuals, even when the crowd drowns them out.

As dramatic as this scene is so far, what happens next is a showstopper. We know the crowd is watching Bartimaeus intently now that Jesus has called for him to come near. Without hesitation, Bartimaeus throws off his coat and does what Jesus asks. For a blind man in the first century, the coat was typically spread out in front of him to collect spare change. As the crowd watches, Bartimaeus abandons what is likely his only possession and the sole means of getting enough money to stay alive. He has total confidence that Jesus will give him eyes to see.

When Jesus askes him, "What do you want me to do for you?" Bartimaeus answers with emotion and reverence, addressing Jesus as "My Rabbi." A faith like this that is eager, persistent, obedient, personal, and ultimately self-abandoning will lead to healing and ultimately to salvation.

A BIBLICAL EMBRACE OF
THE SUPERNATURAL...TODAY

After Bartimaeus is healed, he follows Jesus on the road. When we are healed, whether physically or spiritually, we must continue to follow Jesus no matter what.

DAY 18

The Miraculous Catch of Fish

LUKE 5:1-10

One day as Jesus was preaching on the shore of the Sea of Galilee, great crowds pressed in on him to listen to the word of God. He noticed two empty boats at the water's edge, for the fishermen had left them and were washing their nets. Stepping into one of the boats, Jesus asked Simon, its owner, to push it out into the water. So he sat in the boat and taught the crowds from there.

When he had finished speaking, he said to Simon, "Now go out where it is deeper, and let down your nets to catch some fish."

"Master," Simon replied, "we worked hard all last night and didn't catch a thing. But if you say so, I'll let the nets down again." And this time their nets were so full of fish they began to tear! A shout for help brought their partners in the other boat, and soon both boats were filled with fish and on the verge of sinking.

When Simon Peter realized what had happened, he fell to his knees before Jesus and said, "Oh, Lord, please leave me—I'm such a sinful man." For he was awestruck by the number of fish they had caught, as were the others with him. His partners, James and John, the sons of Zebedee, were also amazed.

Jesus replied to Simon, "Don't be afraid! From now on you'll be fishing for people!"

GOING TO
WHERE IT IS DEEPER

In a supernatural world inhabited by a supernatural God, this story of Jesus and the miraculous catch of fish reminds us that God has power over nature. As God in human form, Jesus commands and interrupts nature—the very definition of a miracle—several times during his three-year ministry on earth. In this story he fills the nets of two boats with so many fish the boats nearly sink.

When Peter realizes that he is in the presence of Jesus Christ, the Lord of heaven and earth, he falls to his knees and asks forgiveness. This reaction echoes the terrified response of the disciples when Jesus calms the storm (Mark 4:35-41) and walks on water (Mark 6:47-50). When we experience the miraculous work of God in our world and our lives, we need to recognize not only God's power, but also our own unworthiness.

Despite our flaws and lack of trust, God calls us and uses us in his service. But he doesn't leave us where we are. Instead, he tells us, "Now go out to where it is deeper." This is where the fish are. The deep is where the Holy Spirit can give us power in service to Jesus, the Lord of the harvest (Matthew 9:38).

A BIBLICAL EMBRACE OF
THE SUPERNATURAL...TODAY

In the deep is where we see God's miraculous work to bring people to his Son. The deep is where we fish for those who are lost.

DAY 19

Jesus Heals a Man
with Leprosy

Luke 5:12-16

In one of the villages, Jesus met a man with an advanced case of leprosy. When the man saw Jesus, he bowed with his face to the ground, begging to be healed. "Lord," he said, "if you are willing, you can heal me and make me clean."

Jesus reached out and touched him. "I am willing," he said. "Be healed!" And instantly the leprosy disappeared. Then Jesus instructed him not to tell anyone what had happened. He said, "Go to the priest and let him examine you. Take along the offering required in the law of Moses for those who have been healed of leprosy. This will be a public testimony that you have been cleansed."

But despite Jesus' instructions, the report of his power spread even faster, and vast crowds came to hear him preach and to be healed of their diseases. But Jesus often withdrew to the wilderness for prayer.

JESUS IS WILLING

In the first century, leprosy was considered a contagious, incurable disease, turning its victims into social outcasts. No one dared come into contact with a leper for fear of getting the dreaded disease. That is, no one but Jesus. Not only does Jesus pay attention to this particular leper, but he reaches out and touches him and instantly heals him, showing his compassion as well as his authority over the disease. Again, had the religious leaders been paying attention, they would have known that Jesus is the Messiah described by the prophet Isaiah as one who will cleanse lepers (Matthew 11:5; Isaiah 35:4-6).

That's why Jesus tells the cleansed leper to report to the priest for examination. He wants the priest to know that his work of healing is fulfilling prophecy. At the same time, Jesus is fulfilling the law, which required that lepers who were healed be examined by the priest in order to be declared clean (Leviticus 14:1-32).

Jesus urges the healed man to not tell anyone else about his healing, concerned that people would come to him just for the physical benefits. But as usual with others who were healed, the restored man can't help but express his joy.

A BIBLICAL EMBRACE OF
THE SUPERNATURAL...TODAY

The leper was convinced that Jesus was willing to heal him. Whenever we approach Jesus in prayer, we need to pray the prayer of Jesus to his Father: "Not my will but your will be done."

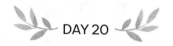

Jesus Forgives and Heals a Paralyzed Man

LUKE 5:17-26

One day while Jesus was teaching, some Pharisees and teachers of religious law were sitting nearby. And the Lord's healing power was strongly with Jesus.

Some men came carrying a paralyzed man on a sleeping mat. They tried to take him inside to Jesus, but they couldn't reach him because of the crowd. So they went up to the roof and took off some tiles. Then they lowered the sick man on his mat down into the crowd, right in front of Jesus. Seeing their faith, Jesus said to the man, "Young man, your sins are forgiven."

But the Pharisees and teachers of religious law said to themselves, "Who does he think he is? That's blasphemy! Only God can forgive sins!"

Jesus knew what they were thinking, so he asked them, "Why do you question this in your hearts? Is it easier to say 'Your sins are forgiven,' or 'Stand up and walk'? So I will prove to you that the Son of Man has the authority on earth to forgive sins." Then Jesus turned to the paralyzed man and said, "Stand up, pick up your mat, and go home!"

And immediately, as everyone watched, the man jumped up, picked up his mat, and went home praising God. Everyone was gripped with great wonder and awe, and they praised God, exclaiming, "We have seen amazing things today!"

THE REASON FOR HEALING

This familiar story of healing is one of the best-known in the entire Bible. There's something about the persistence of the friends of the paralyzed man that captivates us. Indeed, Jesus is impressed with "their faith," but faith isn't the main point of the story. What we are seeing is the primary reason for the healing ministry of Jesus. Yes, the miracles of Jesus show his compassion and power, but even more they demonstrate the authority he has to forgive sins.

You see, physical healing will help us in this life only. But spiritual healing helps for eternity. And spiritual healing—that supernatural process of giving new life to those who are dead in their sins—is possible because Jesus has the authority to forgive sins. Just like every human being before or since, the man's problem isn't physical but spiritual. That's why Jesus starts with forgiveness, the ultimate gift of healing.

Of course, the Pharisees don't buy the first declaration, "Your sins are forgiven," because admitting that Jesus can forgive sins means admitting that he is God, something they are loathe to do. So Jesus provides a second declaration, "Stand up and walk," providing a visible sign of his divine authority.

A BIBLICAL EMBRACE OF
THE SUPERNATURAL...TODAY

Those who witness this miracle give glory to God. This should always be our first response to the healing power of Jesus.

Healing the Centurion's Servant

Luke 7:1-10

When Jesus had finished saying all this to the people, he returned to Capernaum. At that time the highly valued slave of a Roman officer was sick and near death. When the officer heard about Jesus, he sent some respected Jewish elders to ask him to come and heal his slave. So they earnestly begged Jesus to help the man. "If anyone deserves your help, he does," they said, "for he loves the Jewish people and even built a synagogue for us."

So Jesus went with them. But just before they arrived at the house, the officer sent some friends to say, "Lord, don't trouble yourself by coming to my home, for I am not worthy of such an honor. I am not even worthy to come and meet you. Just say the word from where you are, and my servant will be healed. I know this because I am under the authority of my superior officers, and I have authority over my soldiers. I only need to say, 'Go,' and they go, or 'Come,' and they come. And if I say to my slaves, 'Do this,' they do it."

When Jesus heard this, he was amazed. Turning to the crowd that was following him, he said, "I tell you, I haven't seen faith like this in all Israel!" And when the officer's friends returned to his house, they found the slave completely healed.

HEALING IS FOR ANYONE
WHO BELIEVES

There are many stories in the four Gospels where Jesus heals someone or casts out a demon, and the people watching the miraculous event are left in a state of amazement. In this story, Jesus is the one who is amazed.

This story is unique because of the way the healing takes place. There's no indication that Jesus ever meets the Roman officer. Before he arrives at the house, some friends explain that the centurion believes Jesus can heal the servant remotely. This expression of faith amazes Jesus.

"Jesus was pleased with the centurion's faith," writes Matthew Henry. "He never fails to answer the expectations of faith that honor his power and love."[4] We can see where the centurion honors the healing power of Jesus, but how does he honor the love of Jesus?

First by loving those whom Jesus loves—the Jewish people. The centurion is a Gentile, but he demonstrates genuine love by building a synagogue for the very people he oversees. The other way the centurion honors the love of Jesus is by showing concern for his servant, giving us a vivid illustration of what Jesus said: "Whatever you did for one of the least of these...you did for me" (Matthew 25:40 NIV).

A BIBLICAL EMBRACE OF
THE SUPERNATURAL...TODAY

Jesus came especially for "the people of Israel" (Matthew 15:24), but his healing power is all-inclusive. No one who seeks Jesus and has faith to believe will be turned away.

Jesus Raises a Widow's Son

LUKE 7:11-17

Soon afterward Jesus went with his disciples to the village of Nain, and a large crowd followed him. A funeral procession was coming out as he approached the village gate. The young man who had died was a widow's only son, and a large crowd from the village was with her. When the Lord saw her, his heart overflowed with compassion. "Don't cry!" he said.

Then he walked over to the coffin and touched it, and the bearers stopped. "Young man," he said, "I tell you, get up." Then the dead boy sat up and began to talk! And Jesus gave him back to his mother.

Great fear swept the crowd, and they praised God, saying, "A mighty prophet has risen among us," and "God has visited his people today." And the news about Jesus spread throughout Judea and the surrounding countryside.

THE COMPASSION OF JESUS

The large crowd that followed Jesus after he healed the centurion's servant must have been jubilant. Perhaps some in the throng are expectant. Will Jesus heal again? Will he heal me?

The crowd follows Jesus to a nearby village, where they meet a funeral procession about to leave the town in order to bury the son of a widow. She is grief-stricken, and in the crowd of mourners Jesus sees her, "his heart overflowing with compassion." As one commentary states with characteristic elegance,

> What consolation to thousands of the bereaved has this single verse carried from age to age. What mingled majesty and grace shines in this scene. The Resurrection and the life in human flesh, with a word of command, bringing back life to the dead body. Incarnate Compassion summoning its absolute power to dry a widow's tears.[5]

Jesus then touches the bier, a ceremoniously unclean object, and calls out to the young man, telling him to get up. And so he does, immediately speaking, perhaps giving glory to God. The crowd is overcome with fear, having witnessed the might and compassion of God.

A BIBLICAL EMBRACE OF
THE SUPERNATURAL...TODAY

This same Jesus, who brings the dead to life, can also touch our dead souls and raise us to spiritual life.

Jesus Turns Water into Wine

JOHN 2:1-11

The next day there was a wedding celebration in the village of Cana in Galilee. Jesus' mother was there, and Jesus and his disciples were also invited to the celebration. The wine supply ran out during the festivities, so Jesus' mother told him, "They have no more wine."

"Dear woman, that's not our problem," Jesus replied. "My time has not yet come." But his mother told the servants, "Do whatever he tells you."

Standing nearby were six stone water jars, used for Jewish ceremonial washing. Each could hold twenty to thirty gallons. Jesus told the servants, "Fill the jars with water." When the jars had been filled, he said, "Now dip some out, and take it to the master of ceremonies." So the servants followed his instructions.

When the master of ceremonies tasted the water that was now wine, not knowing where it had come from (though, of course, the servants knew), he called the bridegroom over. "A host always serves the best wine first," he said. "Then, when everyone has had a lot to drink, he brings out the less expensive wine. But you have kept the best until now!"

This miraculous sign at Cana in Galilee was the first time Jesus revealed his glory. And his disciples believed in him.

A FORETASTE OF
THE JOY OF HEAVEN

Because Jesus encountered so many sick and desperate people during his earthly sojourn, you could easily conclude that he was all business, with little time for recreation or fun. Yet if the miracle of turning water into wine is any indication, Jesus not only valued joy, but was also pretty good at providing joy for others.

What I like about this miracle is the emphasis on the excellence of what God provides for his children. It's no accident that Jesus chooses a wedding for his first public appearance and his first miracle. Weddings were joyous occasions in the first century as they are today, only in those days a wedding celebration would last for days. Wine was a key element, so running out before the wedding ended created a huge embarrassment for the bridegroom.

That's when Jesus steps in and miraculously turns six jars of water into the finest wine anybody had ever tasted. Of course, there was an earthly, physical benefit to this miracle. The wedding was not just salvaged, but also made considerably better. Oh, how the joy must have flowed!

There was also a heavenly message in the miracle. While the water represents our earthly existence, the wine is a sign of the abundance and joy that awaits us in heaven.

A BIBLICAL EMBRACE OF
THE SUPERNATURAL...TODAY

Upon witnessing this miracle, the disciples believed in Jesus. Let us never forget that the purpose of the supernatural work of God is to encourage belief in his Son.

DAY 24

Jesus Raises Lazarus from the Dead

JOHN 11:38-46

Jesus was still angry as he arrived at the tomb, a cave with a stone rolled across its entrance. "Roll the stone aside," Jesus told them.

But Martha, the dead man's sister, protested, "Lord, he has been dead for four days. The smell will be terrible."

Jesus responded, "Didn't I tell you that you would see God's glory if you believe?"

So they rolled the stone aside. Then Jesus looked up to heaven and said, "Father, thank you for hearing me. You always hear me, but I said it out loud for the sake of all these people standing here, so that they will believe you sent me."

Then Jesus shouted, "Lazarus, come out!" And the dead man came out, his hands and feet bound in grave clothes, his face wrapped in a headcloth.

Jesus told them, "Unwrap him and let him go!"

Many of the people who were with Mary believed in Jesus when they saw this happen. But some went to the Pharisees and told them what Jesus had done.

THE POWER OF
GOD'S VOICE

There are two characteristics of this famous miracle that stand out. First is the anger Jesus displays before raising Lazarus back to life. Notice that he was angry before he arrived at the scene, not at the people or even the circumstances that led to the death of Lazarus, but at death itself.

The other aspect to this miracle is the power of God's voice. Jesus raises a dead man to life merely by the sound of his voice. And it's not just the volume of the "shout" that matters. It is the power of that voice that causes the miracle. A lifeless body can't hear, but God's voice can raise the dead.

Shortly before this miracle, Jesus tells some Jews, "My sheep hear my voice, and I know them, and they follow me" (John 10:27 ESV). Lazarus was a follower of Jesus, so when Jesus tells him to come out of the grave, he knows what to do. As dramatic as this moment is, it's only a foretaste of what it will be like when Jesus returns to earth to bring to life the believers who have died. As he did with Lazarus, he will raise them from the dead "with a commanding shout" (1 Thessalonians 4:16).

A BIBLICAL EMBRACE OF
THE SUPERNATURAL...TODAY

Death will be the last enemy to be defeated (1 Corinthians 15:26), so this demonstration of supernatural power over that enemy provides a preview of what we can expect when we die.

The Empty Tomb

JOHN 20:1-12

Early on Sunday morning, while it was still dark, Mary Magdalene came to the tomb and found that the stone had been rolled away from the entrance. She ran and found Simon Peter and the other disciple, the one whom Jesus loved. She said, "They have taken the Lord's body out of the tomb, and we don't know where they have put him!"

Peter and the other disciple started out for the tomb. They were both running, but the other disciple outran Peter and reached the tomb first. He stooped and looked in and saw the linen wrappings lying there, but he didn't go in. Then Simon Peter arrived and went inside. He also noticed the linen wrappings lying there, while the cloth that had covered Jesus' head was folded up and lying apart from the other wrappings. Then the disciple who had reached the tomb first also went in, and he saw and believed—for until then they still hadn't understood the Scriptures that said Jesus must rise from the dead. Then they went home.

Mary was standing outside the tomb crying, and as she wept, she stooped and looked in. She saw two white-robed angels, one sitting at the head and the other at the foot of the place where the body of Jesus had been lying.

EXPECT THE UNEXPECTED

The miracle of the empty tomb is the one supernatural event upon which all other miracles depend. Without the risen Christ, the supernatural collapses into a black hole and all hope is gone. On the other hand, with the reality of the empty tomb comes the ultimate hope for all humanity.

I love the way the Bible tells stories because it presents the truth, even if it doesn't meet our expectations. You would expect one or more of Jesus' disciples to be the first ones at the tomb on Easter morning, but it's Mary and some other women who are there first. These are likely the same women who stood at the foot of the cross as Jesus died.

When Peter and John (the one Jesus loved and the author of this story) arrive at the scene, you would expect them to believe Christ is risen as soon as they see the stone rolled away. After all, weren't they expecting this miracle? Did not Jesus tell them that he would rise from the dead after three days? He did, but they failed to believe. It took a second piece of evidence—the grave clothes laying as if the body they covered had suddenly disappeared—to convince them that their Savior had indeed risen as he said he would.

A BIBLICAL EMBRACE OF
THE SUPERNATURAL...TODAY

Peter and John immediately leave, missing the drama to come. Mary lingered, weeping, and looked inside the tomb where two angels sat. Next, she would see Jesus himself.

Peter and the Crippled Beggar

ACTS 3:1-10

Peter and John went to the Temple one afternoon to take part in the three o'clock prayer service. As they approached the Temple, a man lame from birth was being carried in. Each day he was put beside the Temple gate, the one called the Beautiful Gate, so he could beg from the people going into the Temple. When he saw Peter and John about to enter, he asked them for some money.

Peter and John looked at him intently, and Peter said, "Look at us!" The lame man looked at them eagerly, expecting some money. But Peter said, "I don't have any silver or gold for you. But I'll give you what I have. In the name of Jesus Christ the Nazarene, get up and walk!"

Then Peter took the lame man by the right hand and helped him up. And as he did, the man's feet and ankles were instantly healed and strengthened. He jumped up, stood on his feet, and began to walk! Then, walking, leaping, and praising God, he went into the Temple with them.

All the people saw him walking and heard him praising God. When they realized he was the lame beggar they had seen so often at the Beautiful Gate, they were absolutely astounded!

GIVE WHAT YOU HAVE

The story is an example of God's kingdom breaking into this world. Our spiritual senses are awakened when this happens. As the people see the lifelong cripple "walking, leaping and praising God," they are absolutely astounded. Remember this as you go about your day. People are waiting for the touch of God as you pass by them. They are looking for the breakthrough of the kingdom of God. They just don't know it yet.

How can we be used of God in this way? First, we need to be intentional and available. Peter and John don't bypass the crippled beggar. They give him the dignity of looking at him "intently." And they take time to stop and address the man. We need to be tuned to God's timing. We are always in a hurry, but God has time for everyone.

Second, we need to give what we have. We may not have money or even profound words, but "we must see that we have something to give to a paralyzed and perishing world."[6] That gift is Jesus. "The Savior makes us able to walk and leap in God's ways."[7] No doubt the onlookers are familiar with the healings of Jesus, but they are still astounded, perhaps because they see his power at work in these ordinary followers of Christ.

A BIBLICAL EMBRACE OF
THE SUPERNATURAL...TODAY

The Beautiful Gate was renowned for its splendor, but it had no power. Only the beauty of our Savior brings healing life to a lost and broken humanity.

Peter's Vision

ACTS 10:9-16

The next day as Cornelius's messengers were nearing the town, Peter went up on the flat roof to pray. It was about noon, and he was hungry. But while a meal was being prepared, he fell into a trance. He saw the sky open, and something like a large sheet was let down by its four corners. In the sheet were all sorts of animals, reptiles, and birds. Then a voice said to him, "Get up, Peter; kill and eat them."

"No, Lord," Peter declared. "I have never eaten anything that our Jewish laws have declared impure and unclean."

But the voice spoke again: "Do not call something unclean if God has made it clean." The same vision was repeated three times. Then the sheet was suddenly pulled up to heaven.

Peter was very perplexed. What could the vision mean? Just then the men sent by Cornelius found Simon's house. Standing outside the gate, they asked if a man named Simon Peter was staying there.

Meanwhile, as Peter was puzzling over the vision, the Holy Spirit said to him, "Three men have come looking for you. Get up, go downstairs, and go with them without hesitation. Don't worry, for I have sent them."

WHEN GOD USES
DREAMS AND VISIONS

Peter was a stubborn and impulsive man. He insisted that Jesus didn't have to die, a statement that invoked a swift and harsh rebuke from Jesus (Matthew 16:22-23). But Peter was also loyal and perceptive. When he declared Jesus to be the Messiah, Jesus praised him (Matthew 16:15-18).

Here we see Peter falling asleep and seeing a vision. It's a strange dream with a clear message. In Christ there is no longer any separation between Jew or Gentile, slave or free, or men and women (Galatians 3:28). God tells Peter through the vision that he doesn't have to follow Jewish restrictions based on the law of Moses. "The old life is gone; a new life has begun!" (2 Corinthians 5:17). Besides, as Jesus said, it isn't what goes into your mouth that defiles you, but the words that come out (Matthew 15:11).

Peter learns this crucial lesson through a dream. Sometimes this is how God talks to us. Usually he speaks to us through his Word, through the inner voice of the Holy Spirit, and through wise counselors. But God also uses dreams and visions—what Dallas Willard calls "a form of divine communication"—to talk to us.[8]

A BIBLICAL EMBRACE OF
THE SUPERNATURAL...TODAY

Most of our dreams are quite ordinary, but occasionally God will interrupt our sleep with something that can only be classified as supernatural. So stay alert, even when you are asleep!

DAY 28

Paul and Barnabas
Are Called Gods

ACTS 14:8-15

While they were at Lystra, Paul and Barnabas came upon a man with crippled feet. He had been that way from birth, so he had never walked. He was sitting and listening as Paul preached. Looking straight at him, Paul realized he had faith to be healed. So Paul called to him in a loud voice, "Stand up!" And the man jumped to his feet and started walking.

When the crowd saw what Paul had done, they shouted in their local dialect, "These men are gods in human form!" They decided that Barnabas was the Greek god Zeus and that Paul was Hermes, since he was the chief speaker. Now the temple of Zeus was located just outside the town. So the priest of the temple and the crowd brought bulls and wreaths of flowers to the town gates, and they prepared to offer sacrifices to the apostles.

But when the apostles Barnabas and Paul heard what was happening, they tore their clothing in dismay and ran out among the people, shouting, "Friends, why are you doing this? We are merely human beings—just like you! We have come to bring you the Good News that you should turn from these worthless things and turn to the living God, who made heaven and earth, the sea, and everything in them."

TURN TO THE LIVING GOD

The man Paul and Barnabas heal had been crippled since birth, just like the lame man Peter and John heal in Acts 3 at the Beautiful Gate. In both cases, before the man could instantly jump to his feet and walk, God had to restore bone and muscle mass.

When the onlookers see this miracle, they are stunned and worked into a kind of frenzy, quickly deciding that the two apostles are gods. A local legend in Lystra says that the gods Zeus and Hermes visited this very region, so the people conclude that these gods have returned and are standing right in front of them. They begin making preparations to worship and offer sacrifices to Paul and Barnabas.

Often we think that those who don't know Jesus have little interest in the supernatural. Just the opposite is true. People without knowledge of the one true God are desperate to make a connection between the natural and the supernatural. They are lost and ignorant and don't even know it. That's why Paul and Barnabas react the way they do. Of course, they are mortified that people would want to worship them. Instead, their hope is that the people of Lystra would turn away from "these worthless things and turn to the living God."

A BIBLICAL EMBRACE OF
THE SUPERNATURAL...TODAY

Whenever you see God referred to as "the living God" in Scripture, it stands as an affirmation that he is the supernatural God who created the world and everything in it.

The Return of Jesus

1 Thessalonians 4:13-18

Dear brothers and sisters, we want you to know what will happen to the believers who have died so you will not grieve like people who have no hope. For since we believe that Jesus died and was raised to life again, we also believe that when Jesus returns, God will bring back with him the believers who have died.

We tell you this directly from the Lord: We who are still living when the Lord returns will not meet him ahead of those who have died. For the Lord himself will come down from heaven with a commanding shout, with the voice of the archangel, and with the trumpet call of God.

First, the believers who have died will rise from their graves. Then, together with them, we who are still alive and remain on the earth will be caught up in the clouds to meet the Lord in the air. Then we will be with the Lord forever. So encourage each other with these words.

A GLORIOUS DAY

Like Christians today, Christians in the first century were convinced that Jesus was going to return to earth a second time. Like us, they didn't know *when* he would return, but before Paul wrote this letter, they didn't know what would happen to their fellow believers who died before Jesus came back.

In order to relieve them of their anxiety so they wouldn't grieve like people without hope, Paul explains the process in an explicit, orderly way. If you've been a Christian for a while, you have no doubt read this passage. And it should give you hope—for your loved ones who have died, as well as for yourself.

The reason Paul can confidently provide this explanation is because of the resurrection of Jesus. Without the empty tomb, we are hopeless and helpless. But the tomb is empty, and Jesus will return as surely as the sun rises, announced by three spectacular, supernatural sounds. The third one, the trumpet call of God, should give you shivers. It will be a magnificent call to summon God's people—those who have died first, followed by those who are still alive—to get them ready for their eternal home. What a glorious day that will be!

A BIBLICAL EMBRACE OF
THE SUPERNATURAL...TODAY

To those who will need to be raised when Jesus returns, Jesus is the resurrection. To those who are living on that glorious day, Jesus is the life (John 11:25).

A New Heaven and a New Earth

REVELATION 21:1-7

I saw a new heaven and a new earth, for the old heaven and the old earth had disappeared. And the sea was also gone. And I saw the holy city, the new Jerusalem, coming down from God out of heaven like a bride beautifully dressed for her husband.

I heard a loud shout from the throne, saying, "Look, God's home is now among his people! He will live with them, and they will be his people. God himself will be with them. He will wipe every tear from their eyes, and there will be no more death or sorrow or crying or pain. All these things are gone forever."

And the one sitting on the throne said, "Look, I am making everything new!" And then he said to me, "Write this down, for what I tell you is trustworthy and true."

And he also said, "It is finished! I am the Alpha and the Omega—the Beginning and the End. To all who are thirsty I will give freely from the springs of the water of life. All who are victorious will inherit all these blessings, and I will be their God, and they will be my children."

"IT IS FINISHED!"

For the third time in this 30-day devotional journey we read about the voice of God shouting from his throne, this time proclaiming the ultimate fulfillment of the good news of the gospel.

The image of the holy city descending from God is breathtaking. It is the apex of all supernatural events, because once again the supernatural and natural are dwelling together seamlessly, only now the new heaven and new earth are as one.

There will be no need for miracles and healing, for we will be in the very presence of almighty God, where there is no more death or sorrow or crying or pain. God's consummate power and glory will be on full display in the new heaven and new earth. We will be back in Eden, only this time, everything around us will be infinitely better.

Just as the old heaven and old earth will be replaced by a new heaven and a new earth of unimaginable beauty, so our own bodies will be transfigured into those fit for this glorious new place and this eternal existence. The presence of God will not be interrupted as it is now. We will experience continuous joy as we eternally dwell with God the Father, God the Son, and God the Holy Spirit in perfect community, harmony, and beauty.

A BIBLICAL EMBRACE OF
THE SUPERNATURAL...TODAY

When God says, "It is finished!" we remember the same words Jesus spoke on the cross when he died for us, giving us the opportunity to live in the new heaven and new earth forever.

NOTES

Chapter 1: What Is a Miracle?

1. A.W. Tozer, *The Pursuit of God* (Ventura, CA: Regal Books, 2013), 26.

2. Barna Research, "Most Americans Believe in Supernatural Healing," Barna.com, September 29, 2016, www.barna.com/research/americans-believe-supernatural-healing/.

3. Eric Metaxas, *Miracles* (New York: Dutton, 2014), 11.

4. C.S. Lewis, *Miracles* (San Francisco, CA: HarperOne, 2001), 5.

5. Lewis, *Miracles*.

6. Lewis, *Miracles*, 12.

7. Lewis, *Miracles*, 74-75.

8. Norman L. Geisler, *Baker Encyclopedia of Christian Apologetics* (Grand Rapids, MI: Baker Books, 1999), 450.

9. Lewis, *Miracles*, 74.

10. Lewis, *Miracles*, 75.

11. Richard L. Purtill, "Defining Miracles," in *In Defense of Miracles: A Comprehensive Case for God's Action in History*, eds. R. Douglas Geivett and Gary R. Habermas (Downers Grove, IL: InterVarsity Press, 1997), 64.

12. Geisler, *Baker Encyclopedia of Christian Apologetics*, 472.

13. C.S. Lewis, *The Weight of Glory* (San Francisco, CA: HarperOne, 2001), 45.

14. Geisler, *Baker Encyclopedia of Christian Apologetics*, 454.

15. Geisler, *Baker Encyclopedia of Christian Apologetics*, 451.

Chapter 2: Why Don't We Take Miracles and Healing Seriously?

1. C.S. Lewis, *A Grief Observed* (San Francisco, CA: HarperSanFrancisco, 2001), 6.

2. Winfried Corduan, "Recognizing a Miracle," in *In Defense of Miracles*, R. Douglas Geivett and Gary Habermas, eds. (Downers Grove, IL: InterVarsity Press Academic, 1997), 104.

3. Corduan, "Recognizing a Miracle," *In Defense of Miracles*, 105.

4. Geisler, *Baker Encyclopedia of Christian Apologetics* (Grand Rapids, MI: Baker Books, 1999), 469.

5. Geisler, *Baker Encyclopedia of Christian Apologetics*, 469-70.

6. Dallas Willard, *Hearing God* (Downers Grove, IL: InterVarsity Press, 2012), 142.

7. Jack Deere, *Surprised by the Voice of God* (Grand Rapids, MI: Zondervan, 1996), 255.

8. Deere, *Surprised by the Voice of God*, 261.

9. Willard, *Hearing God*, 44.

10. Willard, *Hearing God*, 45.

11. Eugene Peterson, *Every Step an Arrival* (Colorado Springs, CO: Waterbrook, 2018), 48.

Chapter 3: The Three Greatest Miracles

1. Lee Strobel, *The Case for Miracles* (Grand Rapids, MI: Zondervan, 2018), 61.

2. Bruce Bickel and Stan Jantz, *Creation and Evolution 101* (Eugene, OR: Harvest House, 2001).

3. Guillermo Gonzalez and Jay W. Richards, *The Privileged Planet* (Washington, DC: Regnery, 2004), 334.

4. Lewis, *Miracles* (San Francisco, CA: HarperOne, 2001), 173.

5. Jack Deere, *Surprised by the Power of the Spirit* (Grand Rapids, MI: Zondervan, 1993), 109.

6. Strobel, *The Case for Miracles*, 66.

7. Craig Keener, cited in Strobel, *The Case for Miracles*, 86-87.

8. Bruce Bickel and Stan Jantz, *Knowing God 101* (Eugene, OR: Harvest House Publishers, 1999).

9. Keener, cited in Strobel, *The Case for Miracles*, 87.

Chapter 4: Healing and Miracles Today

1. Craig Keener, "Real Raisings from the Dead or Fake News?" *Christianity Today*, May 17, 2019, www.christianitytoday.com/ct/2019/june/miracles-resurrections-real-raisings-fake-news-keener-afric.html.

2. Keener, cited in Strobel, *A Case for Miracles*, (Grand Rapids, MI: Zondervan, 2018), 115.

3. Keener, cited in Strobel, *A Case for Miracles*, 114-15.

4. The topics in this section are drawn primarily from Jack Deere's *Surprised by the Power of the Spirit* and R.A. Torrey's *Divine Healing*.

5. Elmer Towns, *My Father's Names* (Ventura, CA: Regal Books, 1991), 35.

6. Wayne Grudem, *Systematic Theology* (Grand Rapids, MI: Zondervan, 1994), 730.

7. R.A. Torrey, *Divine Healing* (San Bernadino, CA: CrossReach Publications, 2016), 24.

Chapter 5: When God Does (or Doesn't) Heal

1. Strobel, *The Case for Miracles* (Grand Rapids, MI: Zondervan, 2018), 235.

2. Strobel, *The Case for Miracles*, 250.

3. Deere, *Surprised by the Power of the Spirit* (Grand Rapids, MI: Zondervan, 1993), 123.

4. Deere, *Surprised by the Power of the Spirit*.

5. Kate Bowler, "Death, the Prosperity Gospel and Me," *New York Times*, February 13, 2016, www.nytimes.com/2016/02/14/opinion/sunday/death-the-prosperity-gospel-and-me.html.

6. Zac Davis, Ashlee McKinless, Olga Segura, "Kate Bowler on the Spiritual Myths About Health," *American Magazine*, May 23, 2019, www.americamagazine.org/arts-culture/2019/05/23/kate-bowler-spiritual-myths-about-health.

7. Deere, *Surprised by the Power of the Spirit*, 124.

8. Torrey, *Divine Healing*, 28.

9. Stan Jantz, *Fire and Wind: Unleashing the Power and Presence of the Holy Spirit* (Eugene, OR: Harvest House, 2019).

10. Torrey, *Divine Healing*, 38.

11. Torrey, *Divine Healing*, 40.

12. Torrey, *Divine Healing*, 42.

13. Henry W. Wright, *A More Excellent Way* (New Kensington, PA: Whitaker House, 2009).

14. Neil T. Anderson, *The Bondage Breaker* (Eugene, OR: Harvest House, 2019).

Chapter 6: How to Experience the Healing Power of God

1. Kate Bowler, *Everything Happens for a Reason* (New York: Random House, 2018), 75.

2. Bowler, *Everything Happens for a Reason*, 76.

3. Calvin Miller, *Into the Depths of God* (Minneapolis, MN: Bethany House Publishers, 2000), 96.

4. Miller, *Into the Depths of God*, 122.

5. Miller, *Into the Depths of God*, 128.

6. Miller, *Into the Depths of God*, 129.

7. Jantz, *Fire and Wind: Unleashing the Power and Presence of the Holy Spirit* (Eugene, OR: Harvest House, 2019), 29.

8. James K.A. Smith, "The Gift of Not Knowing," *Image Journal*, Issue 103:4.

9. Willard, *Hearing God* (Downers Grove, IL: InterVarsity Press, 2012), 41.

10. Willard, *Hearing God*, 44.

11. *Immerse* is published by Tyndale House Publishers in alliance with the Institute for Bible Reading, www.ImmerseBible.com.

12. Willard, *Hearing God*, 39.

13. Willard, *Hearing God*.

14. Alistair Begg, *Pray Big* (Epsom, Surrey, England: The Good Book Company, 2019), 30.

15. Begg, *Pray Big*, 31.

16. Willard, *Hearing God*, 228-32.

17. J.P. Moreland, *Kingdom Triangle* (Grand Rapids, MI: Zondervan, 2007), 182.

18. Moreland, *Kingdom Triangle*, 182-83.

Chapter 7: A Biblical Embrace of the Supernatural...Today

1. Matthew Henry, *Matthew Henry's Concise Commentary on the Whole Bible* (Nashville, TN: Thomas Nelson, 1997), 336.

2. Henry, *Matthew Henry's Concise Commentary*, 340.

3. Henry, *Matthew Henry's Concise Commentary*, 813.

4. Henry, *Matthew Henry's Concise Commentary*, 950.

5. Robert Jamieson, A.R. Fausset, and David Brown, *Commentary on the Whole Bible* (Grand Rapids, MI: Zondervan, 1973), 999.

6. F.B. Meyer, *F.B. Meyer Bible Commentary* (Wheaton, IL: Tyndale House, 1979), 485.

7. Meyer, *F.B. Meyer Bible Commentary*.

8. Willard, *Hearing God*, 123.

Also by Stan Jantz

Fire and Wind

Scripture tells us that the Holy Spirit dwells in every believer (Ephesians 1:13). Because of that promise, you have an Advocate in your life to guide, help, counsel, and convict you as you live and grow into deeper spiritual truths.

Are you making the most of all the Holy Spirit offers to you? If you yearn to know more about who He is and the powerful ways He can work in your life, *Fire and Wind* will introduce you to...

- the different ways the Spirit ministers to you
- what it means to experience the presence, filling, and power of the Spirit
- how the Spirit guides and teaches you
- the spiritual gifts given to you for the benefit of others
- the inner joy the Spirit makes available to every believer

As you welcome the Holy Spirit, He can make everything about Jesus a reality for you today and every day by His constant presence in and through you.

To learn more about Harvest House books and
to read sample chapters, visit our website:

www.harvesthousepublishers.com

HARVEST HOUSE PUBLISHERS
EUGENE, OREGON